NOODLES

by

SUSAN SLACK

Illustrations by
Michelle Burchard

HPBooks
a division of
PRICE STERN SLOAN
Los Angeles

Cover photo and food styling by Burke/Triolo Photography
Published by HPBooks
a division of Price Stern Sloan, Inc.
11150 Olympic Boulevard
Los Angeles, California 90064
©1993 Susan Slack
Cover photo and illustrations ©1993 Price Stern Sloan, Inc.

Library of Congress Cataloging-in-Publication Data

Slack, Susan Fuller.
    Noodles / by Susan Slack.
       p.cm.
    Includes index.
    ISBN 1-55788-060-3 : $8.95
      1. Cookery (Pasta)I. Title.
TX809.M17S59   1993
641.8'22—dc20   92-44769
                                                      CIP

Printed in the United States of America

10 9 8 7 6 5 4 3 2 1

NOTICE: The information in this book is true and complete to the best of our knowledge. All recommendations are made without any guarantees on the part of the author or Price Stern Sloan. The author and publisher disclaim all liability in connection with the use of this information.

This book is printed on acid-free paper.

Table of Contents

Introduction

What food is chic, sometimes frivolous, but always versatile and delicious? It could only be pasta, everyone's favorite fare! The word pasta is Italian and means "paste." It is a blanket term for all noodles, spaghetti and macaroni. Almost all pasta is known by its Italian name. Although there are hundreds of types of pasta, I have chosen to unravel the mysteries of several types of long winding ribbon noodles, twisting Chinese noodles and stringy spaghetti. You will find recipes for chuka soba, spaghetti, udon, linguini, Chinese egg noodles, vermicelli, cappellini, tagliatelle, kishimen, pappardelle and fusilli. Then there are recipes for the unique whisker-thin noodles made from bean threads and rice noodles. There are also recipes for using noodle doughs to make bite-size Oriental dumplings and rolled pastries.

Once considered the workhorse of peasant diets, noodles and spaghetti are now eaten by everyone. They have become the international favorite food of the chic and trendy. Dieters used to believe they were strictly to be avoided because they were fattening carbohydrates. Now that we know they are healthy, easy-to-digest, complex-carbohydrate foods, we have given them a place of importance in our diets. Athletes consider them the food of champions. One cup cooked, plain egg noodles has 200 calories; 1 cup of eggless pasta has less than 150 calories.

For all their popularity, there is still some confusion over what constitutes a noodle and a spaghetti. And which is the best to buy—fresh or dry?

According to the United States Food and Drug Administration (FDA), noodles must contain wheat flour and egg. Egg noodle dough is cut into flat ribbon shapes, sheets for layering and stuffing, and a host of other fanciful forms. Noodles made from egg dough are generally eaten fresh. Yet dried egg noodles can be purchased in cellophane packages, varying from narrow to extra wide.

Spaghetti is the long edible thread which has twisted itself around the heart of many of the world's cuisines. This reoccurring thread comes in a fat hollow version called bucatini or in several thinner versions such as spaghettini, vermicelli or ultra-fine angel's hair. Spaghetti is made from a hard-wheat (durum) flour and does not contain egg. Look for top-quality imported and domestic brands made from 100% durum wheat or pure semolina. If spaghetti or other types of dried pasta are not made from durum wheat, they quickly become mushy and deteriorate while cooking. They can contain excess starch that can cause the cooking water to boil over the sides of the pot.

In the Orient, pasta is always referred to as noodles. Wheat noodles can be made with egg or without egg. Although domestic noodles must contain egg, the FDA recently ruled that imported Oriental noodle manufacturers can call their eggless wheat products by the name "noodles." Yet, many packages of eggless noodles still come into this country bearing the words, "alimentary paste" or "imitation noodles." Most dried market brands are made without egg.

Besides wheat, Oriental noodles can be made from other flours such as buckwheat. Their flavors and textures differ from American and Italian noodles. Most dried products are usually of good quality. To buy the freshest products, shop in Oriental markets with a high turnover.

Oriental noodles are also made from rice, beans, peas, corn, yams and even cornstarch. Mung bean noodles or bean threads and rice stick noodles are as popular as wheat noodles.

People ask me if I prefer dried packaged pasta or fresh homemade pasta. The answer is that I enjoy both! Some people will eat only imported pasta; others prefer homemade. From my experience, both are excellent products as long as they are top-quality. Try the imported Italian and top-quality domestic kinds made from hard durum wheat, grown especially for making pasta. The imported packages should read "semolina." If it says farina, it means wheat flour. Refined durum wheat is high in the protein gluten which gives dough elasticity. This pasta will have a good flavor and strong texture and is all that good pasta should be.

My favorite fresh noodles are the Oriental egg noodles from Chinatown or from my own kitchen. Many Oriental markets sell soft, fresh skinny coils of noodles from large open boxes or plastic bags. Fresh noodles of all kinds are easy to make. Get your family and guests involved; they will enjoy kneading and rolling the dough.

The main difference in preparation between fresh and dry noodles is the cooking time. Fresh noodles can cook in 1 to 3 minutes, depending on their size. You must watch them every minute they cook. Dry noodles take longer, perhaps as long as 10 to 12 minutes.

In supermarkets, fresh noodles and pasta are often available in a dazzling array of flavors such as lemon, hot chile, cracked pepper, spinach and tomato. You can often find the best noodles and pasta among ethnic groups living throughout the country. Dried noodles are available in every color and flavor of the rainbow. Health food stores carry a good variety of dried noodles like fat-free ramen, whole-wheat noodles and colorful vegetable noodles. Unlike nutty-tasting whole-wheat pasta, white flour and semolina noodles lack germ and bran so they will keep for a longer period.

The recipes in this book are made to serve three or four as a main dish but they can be increased to serve more. Never double the salt amounts; taste first to determine the need for seasoning. Many types of noodles and spaghetti are interchangeable. Feel free to experiment with what you have on hand. There are few hard and fast rules. The main ones are—don't overcook the pasta! And keep a spirit of adventure and a willingness for spontaneous improvisation!

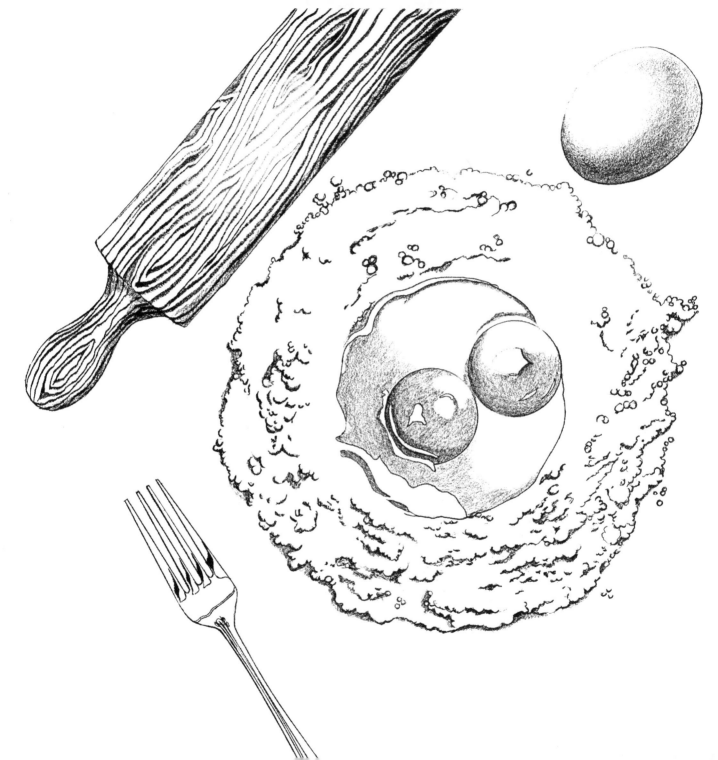

Basic Recipes

Fresh pasta has a special homemade taste and silky smooth texture. It is made with egg, flour and sometimes a little oil. Homemade noodles are much softer than commercial hard-wheat noodles. This doesn't mean one is better than the other. They are simply different products, often used in different ways.

Noodle-making is a traditional art, requiring a little practice to learn how to roll and stretch out the dough the proper way. In Europe and Asia where pride of craftsmanship is high, skilled cooks spend lots of time practicing the art. Fortunately, we have welcomed the food processor and pasta machine into our kitchens as marvelous energy and time-saving devices. Homemade noodles can be cooked and on the table in less than an hour. Here are a few tips which will guide you to success when making your own noodles.

A wooden or Formica surface is good for rolling noodle dough. Marble, granite and solid surfacing materials keep the dough cool, tightening it and making rolling more difficult. If you use one of these, let the dough "relax" for a longer period between mixing and rolling.

Use all-purpose flour or unbleached all-purpose flour for the dough. Bags of semolina pasta flour are now available in many fine grocery stores. Semolina flour mixed with water makes a firm-textured noodle with plenty of "bite." Always use Grade A large eggs. Eggs with deep yellow yolks enhance the dough color.

The amount of eggs or liquid needed to turn flour into a smooth, elastic dough can vary, depending on conditions such as the flour's moisture content and the egg size. If the dough seems sticky, work in one or two tablespoons flour. Too dry, sprinkle in water a teaspoon at a time. Dry the pasta sheets on clean terry cloth towels to help absorb moisture. If too wet, the noodle strands will not separate when cut. Too dry, the dough sheets will crack.

For the best results, try to cook the noodles the same day they are made. If you wish, prepare them in the morning, dry for several hours, then cook the noodles in the evening. A wooden drying rack is handy for hanging the noodles to dry. If stored on baking sheets a few hours, cover lightly with a clean cloth. For longer storage, refrigerate noodles two or three days in an airtight plastic bag or freeze up to two months. Or, dry the noodles at room temperature at least 24 hours, turning one or two times for even drying. Store in an airtight container two to three months.

Making Noodle Dough by Hand

Use this technique for making noodle doughs, including those in this chapter. Place the suggested amount of flour in a shallow mound on a work surface. Make a deep well in the center; add eggs, salt and oil, if used. With a fork, beat the eggs with a circular motion, gradually incorporating the surrounding flour into the egg mixture. If water is called for, add in small amounts as you mix the dough. When the dough begins to holds its shape, work in remaining flour with your hands. Add a few drops of water if too dry or 1 to 2 tablespoons flour if too moist. On a lightly floured surface, knead dough with the heel of your hand 8 to 10 minutes or until smooth and elastic. Cover dough; let it rest from 30 to 60 minutes. Roll out and cut dough by hand or with a pasta machine. To roll by hand, pat dough into a flat shape. With the rolling pin, roll from the center outward, then from the center back. Apply more force when rolling outward in order to stretch the dough. Rotate the dough slightly after each completed roll, until you have a round sheet, 1/8 inch thick. Dust dough on both sides with flour; let dry 10 minutes. Fold over both sides of dough so they meet; cut into strips of desired width. Or, roll up, jelly-roll style, and cut into strips. Toss noodles to loosen; dust lightly with flour. Dry noodles at least 10 minutes before cooking.

Homemade Rice Noodles

These tender, chewy noodle sheets are a substitute for commercial steamed rice noodle sheets, difficult to find outside large Asian communities. Chinese home cooks make similar noodle sheets with cake flour and water. Some add a portion of wheat starch without gluten or tapioca starch made from the cassava plant. Noodle sheets can be filled and rolled, or cut into noodles for soups and stir-frying. These noodles are not as firm and elastic as regular rice noodles, but they are a good substitute.

1 cup cake flour (no substitute)
2 tablespoons cornstarch
1 tablespoon glutinous rice flour
1/2 teaspoon salt
1-1/4 cups water
2 tablespoons vegetable oil plus extra for brushing

Into a medium-size bowl, sift dry ingredients. Whisk in the water and 2 tablespoons of the oil until smooth. In a wok or deep pot, bring water to a boil. Pour 1/3 of the batter into a well-oiled 9-inch-square cake pan. Place pan on a steamer tray; cover. Place over boiling water; steam 2 to 3 minutes or until noodle sheet is dry. Cool completely. Gently turn out of pan onto a lightly oiled surface. Brush top with oil. Steam remaining batter. Do not refrigerate if used the same day. Wrap tightly; refrigerate for longer storage. For noodles, cut into 1/2-inch strips. Makes 3 sheets.

Variation

Fried Rice Noodle Sheets: Increase the amount of cornstarch to 1/2 cup. Add 1/2 cup tapioca starch. Omit rice flour. Increase water to 2 cups. Whisk in water in small amounts. Pour batter into a large nonstick skillet; dry over low heat. Oil sheets well. Or steam as directed above.

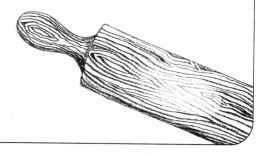

Dragon Noodles

You will hear the roar of the mighty dragon when you taste these vibrant-colored, chile-garlic flavored noodles. Their wonderful flavor can best be appreciated when topped with a simple sauce. These noodles will fire up the heart of every true chile enthusiast; those who can't stand the heat are advised to substitute one tablespoon water for one tablespoon of the fiery chile-garlic sauce.

1-1/2 cups all-purpose flour or unbleached all-purpose flour
1/2 teaspoon salt
1 tablespoon paprika
1 large egg
2 tablespoons chile-garlic sauce (page 110)
2 tablespoons water
1 teaspoon sesame oil
Cornstarch, for dusting

In a food processor with the metal blade, place flour, salt and paprika; process to sift ingredients. In a small bowl, beat egg, chile-garlic sauce, water and sesame oil with a fork. Add to flour; process until dough is crumbly and forms moist clumps. Gather dough on a cornstarch-dusted surface; knead 30 seconds to form a smooth ball. Divide into 4 pieces. Cover; let rest 30 minutes. Flatten 1 piece into an oval shape. Pass through the widest roller setting of a pasta machine (number 1). Fold ends of dough to meet. Feed through the roller, beginning at the unfolded end. Repeat folding and rolling process 5 times. Narrow roller by turning the notch to the next setting (number 2). Feed through roller, unfolded. Continue process, changing the notch each time to narrow the roller. The final roll will be on the second to the last setting (number 5) for a noodle sheet 1/8 inch thick. Roll remaining dough. Dry dough sheets 10 minutes. Coat with cornstarch. Feed through the wide cutting blade to form fettuccine, about 1/4 inch wide. Or, feed through the narrow cutting blade to form a round noodle. In a large pot, bring 3 quarts water to a boil; add noodles. Cook 1 minute or until tender yet firm to the bite. Drain; rinse under cool water. Drain well. Serve in deep bowls with sauce or use for fried noodle dishes. Makes about 12 ounces noodles.

Japanese Udon

*Té-uchi udon, or handmade noodles, are a wheat noodle of substance.
The simple flavor of the white, chewy thick noodle is a favorite in Japan. Special flour for
making udon can be purchased from many Asian markets. It is a special blend of unbleached
white flours. If made by hand, be sure to knead the dough a minimum of ten minutes to achieve
udon's special texture. In Japan, the stiff dough is kneaded by foot! Serve noodles in soup,
with dipping sauce or in one-pot dishes. The noodles are cooked by the shimizu method,
which means cold water is periodically added as the noodles cook.*

2 cups unbleached all-purpose flour
2 teaspoons salt
1/2 cup water

Place flour in a food processor with the metal blade. In a small bowl, dissolve salt in water. Add to flour. Process until dough forms a ball; continue processing 1 minute. Gather dough on a floured surface; knead 4 to 5 minutes. Divide dough in half. Cover; let rest 2 hours or more. Press half the dough into a flat oval shape. Pass through the widest roller setting of a pasta machine (number 1). Fold ends of dough to meet. Feed through roller, beginning at the unfolded end. Repeat rolling and folding process 2 times. Narrow roller by turning the notch to the next setting (number 2). Feed dough through roller, unfolded. Continue process, changing the notch each time to narrow the roller. The final roll should be on the second to the last setting (number 5) for a noodle sheet 1/8 inch thick. Roll remaining dough. Dry dough sheets 10 minutes. Dust with flour. Feed through the narrow cutting blade to form a round noodle, about 1/8 inch wide. Or feed through the wide cutting blade to form flat noodles, about 1/4 inch wide. Dust again with flour. In a large pot, bring 4 quarts water to a boil; add noodles. Stir noodles; bring to a boil. Pour in 1 cup cold water. Bring back to a boil; add 1 cup water. Continue cooking 4 to 5 minutes or until noodles are tender yet slightly firm to the bite. You can add 1 additional cup water at the end of the cooking time. Drain well; rinse under cool water. If noodles cooked ahead need reheating, place in a large strainer and dip into a large pot of boiling water. Refrigerate uncooked noodles up to 3 days or store in the freezer. Makes about 10 ounces.

Variation

Hand-cut Udon: Prepare dough as directed above. Dust dough pieces with flour. With a long thin rolling pin, gently roll and stretch each ball into a rectangular shape, about 1/8 inch thick. Turn several times while rolling; dust with flour. Fold dough into 4 layers, accordion-style. Dust sharp knife with flour; cut into strips from 1/8 inch to 3/8 inch thick, depending on personal preference. Lift and shake out noodles; dust lightly with flour again. Cook as directed above.

Basic Egg Noodles

With the aid of the food processor and pasta machine, you can enjoy fresh Italian-style egg noodles daily. In this recipe, the noodles are cut into tagliatelle or thinner tagliolini. Tagliatelle is similar to fettuccine. Tagliolini can be used in place of spaghetti. Double dough for about one pound of noodles.

2 large eggs
1/2 teaspoon salt plus extra for cooking
1 teaspoon olive oil
1-1/2 cups all-purpose flour

In a food processor with the metal blade, briefly process eggs, the 1/2 teaspoon salt and olive oil. Add flour; process until dough forms a ball. Process dough 30 seconds longer. Divide into 4 pieces. Cover; let rest 30 minutes. Flatten 1 piece into an oval shape. Pass through the widest roller setting of a pasta machine (number 1). Fold ends of dough to meet. Feed through the roller, beginning at the unfolded end. Repeat rolling and folding process five times. Narrow roller by turning the notch to the next setting (number 2). Feed through roller, unfolded. Continue process, changing the notch each time to narrow the roller. The final roll will be on the next to the last setting (number 6) to make a thin noodle sheet, about 1/16 inch thick. Roll remaining dough. Dry dough sheets 10 minutes. Dust with flour. Feed through the wide cutting blade to form a 1/4-inch-wide noodle similar to tagliatelle. Or, through the narrow cutting blade to form thin round noodles. In a large pot, bring 4 quarts water to a boil; add salt and noodles. Cook 1 to 2 minutes or until tender yet firm to the bite. Drain well; serve with desired sauce. Makes about 8 or 9 ounces of noodles.

Variations

If you prefer a slightly thicker noodle, set the roller notch to the second to the last setting (number 5) and roll noodle sheets 1/8 inch thick.

Tomato Tagliatelle: Add 3 tablespoons tomato concentrate (packaged in a tube). Omit 1 egg. Roll and cut dough as directed above.

Chile Tagliatelle: Add 4 teaspoons paprika, 1/2 rounded teaspoon ground red (cayenne) pepper and 1 rounded teaspoon cumin to the flour mixture. Roll and cut dough as directed above.

Lemon-Parsley Tagliatelle: Add 2 tablespoons each grated fresh lemon peel and minced fresh parsley. Roll and cut dough as directed above.

Fresh Herb Tagliatelle: Add 2 tablespoons finely chopped fresh herbs. Roll and cut dough as directed above.

Steamed Noodles: a Chinese Restaurant Trick

The Chinese steam fresh noodles to extend their shelf life and improve their texture after being cooked. Chinese restaurants have long employed this trick for preparing noodles. You can refrigerate steamed noodles for long periods with no loss in flavor or quality. After steaming, they are less likely to fall apart if overcooked. When pan-fried, steamed noodles will have a special, wonderful crispness.

Many commercial noodles, fresh or dried, have been pre-steamed. Look for the noodles with a shiny, glazed appearance and intensified color. Japanese ramen is a good example of steamed noodles. To steam your homemade noodles, spread them over a steamer rack. Place the rack over boiling water; cover tightly. Steam 5 to 8 minutes; steam store-bought fresh noodles slightly longer. Remove noodles; toss to cool and prevent sticking. When completely dry, refrigerate up to 2 weeks or freeze in airtight plastic bags. The noodles can be air-dried and stored several months. Boil noodles 3 to 4 minutes longer than unsteamed noodles. Steamed noodles can be blanched briefly before pan-frying. If thin enough, add them directly to the pan.

Chinese Egg Noodles

*This dough contains less egg than Italian noodles. The light-colored, silky
noodles are excellent in Asian noodle dishes. Use when recipes call for Chinese egg noodles,
Japanese ramen or yaki soba. To make "long-life" noodles, cut the dough in half instead
of four pieces. Note the variation for water dough noodles. Popular in Chinese home cooking,
they are used in soups and topped with meat and vegetable sauces. They are a good choice
for cholesterol-free diets. Double dough for about one pound of noodles.*

1-1/2 cups all-purpose flour
1/2 teaspoon salt
1 large egg
4 tablespoons water
1 teaspoon vegetable oil
Cornstarch, for rolling

In a food processor with the metal blade, add flour, salt and egg. With the machine running, slowly pour in water as needed, processing until dough begins to form into a ball. On a cornstarch-dusted surface, gather dough and knead together 1 minute to form a smooth ball. Divide into 4 pieces. Rub with oil. Cover; let rest 30 minutes. Roll 1 piece into a flat oval shape. Pass through the widest roller setting of a pasta machine (number 1). Fold ends of dough to meet. Feed through the roller, beginning at the unfolded end. Repeat rolling and folding process 3 times. Narrow roller by turning the notch to the next setting (number 2). Feed through roller, unfolded. Continue process, changing the notch each time to narrow the roller. The final roll should be on the second to the last setting (number 5) for a noodle sheet 1/8 inch thick. Dry dough sheets 10 minutes. Coat with cornstarch. Feed through the narrow cutting blade to form a thin round noodle similar to spaghettini. In a large pot bring 3 quarts water to a boil; add noodles. Cook 30 seconds to 1 minute until tender yet firm to the bite. Drain well, rinse under cool water. Drain again. Serve in deep bowls with sauce or broth, or use in fried noodle dishes. Makes about 8 ounces noodles.

Variations

Chinese Water Dough: Prepare basic recipe, omitting egg. Increase water to 6 to 8 tablespoons. Prepare as directed above.

Thin Egg Noodles: Prepare dough as directed above. Turn roller notch to the next to the last setting (number 6) for a noodle sheet about 1/16 inch thick. Cut as directed. Reduce cooking time to 30 seconds.

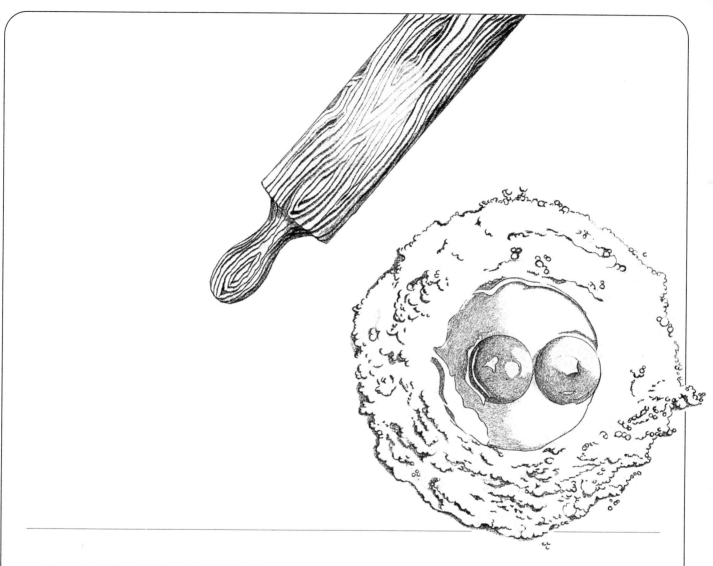

Chocolate Noodle Sheets: Add 1 tablespoon unsweetened cocoa powder and 1/2 teaspoon ground cinnamon. Omit egg; increase water to 5 or 6 tablespoons. Dough needs to be folded and run through the roller only twice. Roll into sheets for use as deep-fried pastry wrappers or cut into noodles for frying.

Sesame Seed Noodles: Add 2 tablespoons white sesame seeds and 1 teaspoon sesame oil. Roll dough and cut into 1/4-inch-wide noodles using the wide cutting blade.

Crespelle

*Crespelle are thin crepelike pancakes popular in Northern and
Central Italian cuisine. They are sometimes used instead of pasta in lasagna
and cannelloni. Crespelle can be stuffed with meat, vegetable or cheese fillings.
Sometimes they are spread with cheese, rolled and placed in the soup bowl.
Cut leftover crespelle into noodlelike strips for soups.*

4 large eggs
1/4 teaspoon salt
1 cup all-purpose flour, sifted
1 cup milk
2 tablespoons butter or olive oil

In a large bowl, beat eggs and salt with a whisk. Beat in flour, a little at a time, alternately with 1 cup milk. Let the batter rest 1 hour. Heat a crepe pan or a 7- or 8-inch nonstick skillet over medium heat. Measure about 2-1/2 tablespoons batter. Melt 1/2 teaspoon butter in the pan; roll pan around. Immediately add batter; roll pan around to evenly coat the bottom with batter. If pan is too hot, batter will burn and not swirl to proper size. Cook 40 seconds or until set and lightly browned. Turn crespella with a spatula; cook 30 seconds on the other side. Remove from pan; place on waxed paper. Repeat with remaining batter. Cooled crespelle can be stacked. Use at once or wrap tightly and refrigerate overnight. Makes 14 crespelle.

Carrot Ribbon Noodles

*Delicate spice-scented carrot noodles are delicious served alone
with butter or mixed with a creamy sauce such as the Wild Mushroom Sauce (page 79).*

---

3 medium-size carrots, sliced
1 large egg
2 cups unbleached all-purpose flour
1/2 teaspoon freshly ground nutmeg
1/2 teaspoon salt
1 teaspoon corn oil

Bring carrots and water to a boil in a medium-size saucepan. Cook until tender; drain well. In a food processor with the metal blade, puree carrots as smoothly as possible. Scrape carrot puree from work bowl. Cool completely. Measure 1/2 cup puree; add back to the work bowl. Add egg; process until mixture is smooth. Add remaining ingredients. Process until dough begins to form into a ball. Gather dough on a lightly floured surface; knead 1 minute to form a smooth ball. Divide into 4 pieces. Cover; let rest 30 minutes. Roll out and cut dough sheets like tagliatelle as directed in Basic Egg Noodles (page 6). Cook as suggested. Toss with desired sauce. Makes about 1 pound pasta.

Variation
Substitute 1/2 cup mashed cooked pumpkin for carrots.

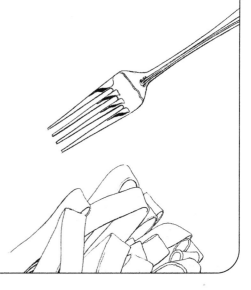

Crispy Won-Ton Vermicelli

These addictive crispy fried noodles are made from deep-fried, ultra-thin won-ton wrappers. They are flavored with seasoned salt and Parmesan cheese. Use them as a crunchy salad or soup topping or grab a handful to eat as a snack on the run!

8 ounces Chinese won-ton wrappers (about 30)
3 cups vegetable oil for deep-frying
Seasoning salt
About 1/2 cup freshly grated Parmesan cheese

For ultra-thin noodles, run each wrapper through the roller of a pasta machine turned to the last setting (number 7). Stack wrappers in bunches. With a large sharp knife, cut into 1/8-inch strips. Heat oil in a wok or heavy, medium-size skillet to 360°F (180°C). Fry noodle shreds in batches, turning several times until crisp and medium golden-brown. Do not fry too fast or noodles will become too dark. Drain on paper towels. Sprinkle seasoning salt and cheese over hot noodles. Cool; serve at once or store in an airtight container up to 2 weeks. Makes 3 or 4 servings.

Variation
Dough sheets can be cut and fried without rolling them through a pasta machine.

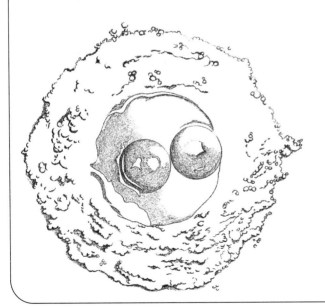

Seven-Spice Powder

This is a tasty Japanese spice blend which will perk up the flavor of any noodle dish, East or West. Grinding the dried pepper is easy if you use a small electric coffee mill.

1-1/2 tablespoons freshly grated orange peel
1 teaspoon toasted sesame seeds
1 teaspoon toasted flax seeds
1 teaspoon toasted poppy seeds
1/2 teaspoon dried sansho-pepper pods, ground to a powder
1/2 cup small dried red chile peppers, seeded, ground to a powder
1/4 teaspoon powdered sea-vegetable mixture (ao-noriko)

Preheat oven to 200°F (95°C). Spread orange peel in a small baking pan. Dry in oven 30 minutes. Put sesame seeds, flax seeds and poppy seeds in a small bowl. With a pestle or similar object, crush seeds gently to release flavor. Stir in orange peel and remaining ingredients. Store in an airtight container. Makes about 1/4 cup.

Korean Red Pepper Sauce

Stir a spoonful of this red pepper sauce into thin Korean wheat noodles or chewy, gelatinous buckwheat noodles. Add julienne strips of fresh or pickled vegetables to create a colorful salad. The sauce is equally good tossed with soba, egg noodles or spaghetti. Use it as a dipping sauce for meats, vegetables and fried tofu.

1 large garlic clove
1 (1/8-inch-thick) slice gingerroot
1 tablespoon toasted sesame seeds
2 tablespoons red wine vinegar
1 tablespoon soy sauce
1 teaspoon sesame oil
1 tablespoon brown sugar
2 tablespoons Korean bean paste (kochu jang)
1/4 teaspoon salt
1/3 cup vegetable oil

In a small food processor, process garlic and gingerroot until finely minced. Add remaining ingredients except oil. With motor running, slowly pour in oil. Makes about 1/2 cup.

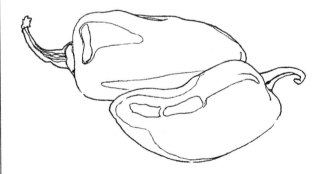

Red Chile Sauce

This fiery Chinese dipping sauce is good with all types of fried,
poached or steamed savory dumplings. Spoon a small amount of sauce over
cooked Asian noodles with sliced vegetables to create a cold noodle salad.

1/2 cup rice vinegar
1 tablespoon soy sauce
1 large garlic clove, finely minced
2 to 3 teaspoons hot chile paste with garlic
1/2 teaspoon toasted sesame oil
2 green onions, minced

In a small bowl, combine all the ingredients. Makes about 1/2 cup.

Garlic & Vinegar Dipping Sauce

This tangy sweet-sour Filipino sauce is good with lumpia and
fried or poached savory dumplings. Make the sauce 30 minutes ahead; the
flavors will taste better and better.

1 cup rice vinegar
1/2 cup water
1/2 cup sugar
3 large garlic cloves, smashed
3 tablespoons ketchup
Pinch salt
1 to 3 teaspoons hot chile sauce

In a small saucepan, stir vinegar, water and sugar over low heat until sugar dissolves. Cool; stir in remaining ingredients. Makes about 1-3/4 cups sauce.

Vietnamese Chile-Lime Dressing

Nuoc-mam is a salty, thin fish sauce used as extensively in Vietnamese cuisine as soy sauce is in China. Its distinctive, pleasant taste subtly enhances the flavors of foods. If you can't find nuoc mam, use nam pla from Thailand. Use this flavorful sauce as a dipping sauce for Oriental fried appetizers or grilled meats, or spoon over green salad, soaked rice vermicelli or bean threads.

1 cup water
1/2 cup Southeast Asian fish sauce (page 111)
1/4 cup fresh lime juice or lemon juice
2 tablespoons sugar
2 large garlic cloves, finely minced
1 small fresh whole red chile pepper, seeded, minced, or 1 to 2 teaspoons chile-garlic sauce
1/2 small carrot, scraped, cut into fine shreds

In a medium-size bowl, combine all ingredients. Use at once or store in an airtight jar in the refrigerator. Makes about 2 cups.

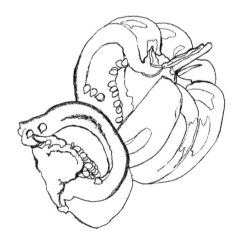

Pineapple Sweet-Sour Sauce

Serve this fruity Oriental sauce with fried spring rolls, lumpia or won tons.

1 cup sugar
1/3 cup ketchup
1/2 cup white vinegar
1/2 teaspoon salt
3 tablespoons cornstarch
1 cup pineapple juice

In a medium-size saucepan, stir together sugar, ketchup, vinegar and salt. In a small bowl, dissolve cornstarch in pineapple juice. Stir into sugar mixture. Place pan over medium-high heat. Cook mixture, stirring often, until it comes to a boil. Cook 30 seconds, stirring constantly, or until mixture thickens. Remove from heat. Serve at once or store at room temperature 3 or 4 hours. Refrigerate leftovers; warm over low heat. Makes about 2-1/2 cups.

Variation
For a spicy version, stir in 1 to 2 teaspoons chile-garlic sauce.

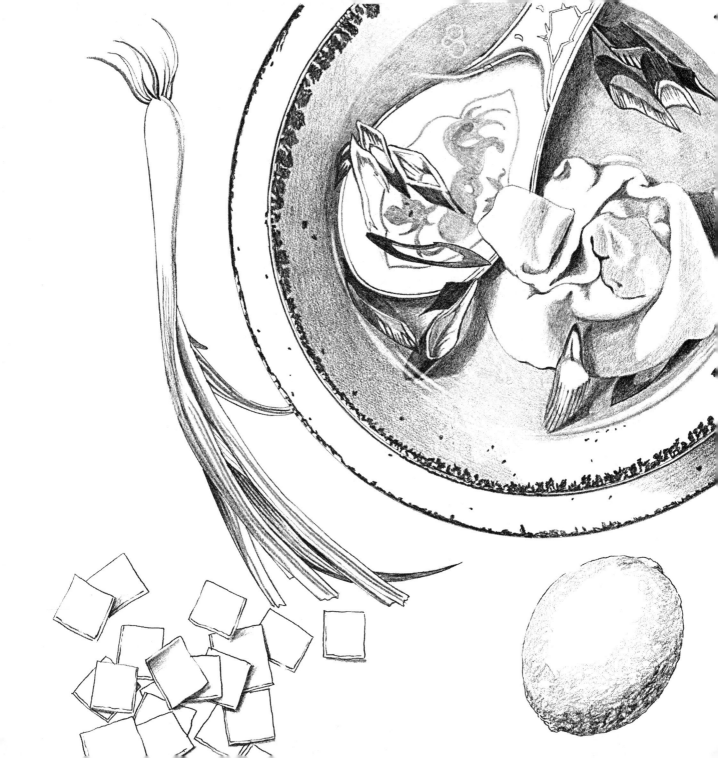

Noodle Soups

Noodle soup is one of the world's most popular comfort foods. It is economical, nutritious and easy to make. Noodle soups can be served as a one-dish meal, a first course or as a hearty snack.

Rich homemade stock is the starting point for making delicious soup. Chicken Stock with Ginger (page 24) is made with a whole chicken, additional chicken parts and aromatic vegetables. Use it in your favorite soup recipes, especially those from the Orient. The stock is simmered for a long period until the flavor is concentrated. There is a bonus in this recipe. The poached meat from the chicken can be removed for use in the soup recipe or saved for another meal. Making stock is easy if you stockpile unused chicken parts and store them in the freezer.

Homemade stock allows the cook great flexibility. Change a few basic ingredients and you create a stock which is very compatible with Western soup recipes. In Japan, the basic soup stock, Dashi (page 23) can be made within minutes from seaweed and dried bonito shavings. Miso Ramen (page 25) is a hearty Japanese noodle soup that is delicious made with chicken stock or Dashi.

In the Orient, soup is everyone's favorite way to eat noodles. It is a popular late-night snack. Noodle soups are served in larger restaurants as part of a multi-course meal. At a Cantonese tea house, they might be served as a filler along with servings of small dim sum snacks. What could be more satisfying for lunch, supper or a midnight snack than a bowl filled with steaming-hot Tea-House Dumpling Soup (page 22)? For added sustenance, place a handful of cooked noodles at the bottom of each soup bowl.

Rich and poor alike, Asians go to local street vendors or hole-in-the-wall noodle houses for a quick snack of noodles with sauce or in soup. The recipe for Copper Well Street Noodles (page 26) is based on a spicy-hot noodle snack from the noodle carts of Tung Ching Street in Szechuan Province.

In China's past, few soup recipes were in circulation, since most people made soup with the ingredients they had on hand. In this spirit, create your own soup recipes with any type of noodles you might have on your kitchen shelf. Long string or ribbon noodles can be broken into smaller pieces before being added to the soup.

Japanese Basket Noodles

In Japan, soba is served in a zaru, or handsome lacquered box with a bamboo plate. A dipping sauce called tsuke-jiru is served on the side. Soba is the original fast food. It is a favorite meal of people too busy to sit down. Experienced connoisseurs can inhale a bowl of soba in record time. Slurping one's noodles is proper etiquette in Japan. It is regarded as absolute proof of enjoyment of the moment!

Condiments, see below
3 cups Dashi (page 23)
3/4 cup soy sauce
3 tablespoons sugar
1/4 cup mirin
1 pound dried soba or other Japanese dried wheat noodles

Condiments:

Crumbled nori (laver seaweed)
2 tablespoons grated fresh gingerroot
8 shredded shiso leaves
4 minced green onions
2 tablespoons wasabi paste
2 tablespoons bonito-thread shavings
2 sheets toasted nori (laver seaweed), cut into short strips

Prepare 2 or 3 Condiments of choice; divide equally among 4 tiny serving dishes. In a medium-size saucepan over low heat, combine Dashi, soy sauce, sugar and mirin to make a dipping sauce. Simmer 3 minutes. For each serving, pour 1 cup dipping sauce in a small bowl. In a large pot, bring 3 quarts water to a boil; add noodles. Cook 4 to 5 minutes or until tender yet slightly firm to the bite. Drain well; rinse under cool water. Drain again. For each serving, pile 1/4 of the noodles on a small basket or plate. Serve with bowls of dipping sauce and Condiments. Diners mix the Condiments into their dipping sauce. Dip each bite of noodles into the sauce before eating. Makes 4 servings.

Chicken Soup with Escarole & Pappardelle

*Fusilli or thick spaghetti broken into two-inch pieces can
be used instead of the wide noodles, pappardelle. For a light meal, serve this
hearty soup with a marinated vegetable salad and hot homemade bread.*

---

8 cups Chicken Stock with Herbs (page 24)
1 tablespoon fresh thyme leaves or 1/2 teaspoon dried leaf thyme
2 tablespoons butter
2 cups packed thin-sliced escarole, Swiss chard or spinach
2 garlic cloves
1/2 teaspoon salt, or to taste
3 to 4 ounces pappardelle, broken into 2-inch pieces
1/4 teaspoon ground white pepper, or to taste
Freshly grated Parmesan cheese

Prepare Chicken Stock with Herbs. Reserve chicken meat. Tear into large pieces. Measure about 2 cups; set aside. Put stock into a medium-size pot over medium heat. Add thyme. In a medium-size saucepan over medium-high heat, melt butter. Add escarole; cook 2 to 3 minutes or until wilted. Add garlic; cook 1 minute more. Stir escarole mixture into soup. Simmer soup, partially covered, 3 or 4 minutes. Bring a medium-size pot of water to a boil; add salt and pappardelle. Cook 4 or 5 minutes or until tender yet firm to the bite. Drain well; add to soup with chicken. Add salt and pepper. When hot, serve in deep bowls; sprinkle with cheese. Makes 4 to 6 servings.

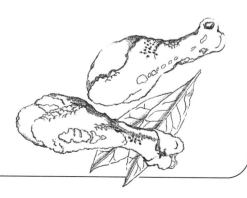

Tea-House Dumpling Soup

Hearty soups filled with stuffed, fat dumplings are served in Asian tea houses, noodle shops and back-alley stalls. Aromas wafting from giant pots of boiling soups, noodles and dumplings are irresistible. These soups are served in large bowls big enough to hold a half dozen dumplings, plus a healthy portion of fresh cooked egg noodles. Serve marinated or pickled vegetables on the side.

---

6 cups Chicken Stock with Ginger (page 24)
1/2 recipe Spicy Chinese Dumplings with Red Chile Sauce (page 88)
1 teaspoon sesame oil
Salt and freshly ground pepper to taste
1 tablespoon light soy sauce
1/4 cup julienned carrots
1/4 cup shredded Virginia ham
2 thinly sliced green onions
4 to 6 ounces Swiss chard or spinach, blanched in boiling water 10 seconds

Prepare Chicken Stock with Ginger. Prepare Spicy Chinese Dumplings with Red Chile Sauce according to recipe directions. Cook dumplings; keep warm. Pour sauce into small bowls for dipping. Heat stock in a large pot over medium-high heat. Add remaining ingredients except Swiss chard; simmer 1 minute. Divide dumplings and Swiss chard into large soup bowls. With a ladle, fill bowls with hot soup. Serve immediately with a spoon for sipping and chopsticks for dipping the dumplings into the spicy sauce. Makes 4 main-dish or 8 first-course servings.

Dashi

Dashi, a mild-tasting stock made from dried sea-vegetable and dried fish shavings, is the basis of many of Japan's famous dishes. It is a flavorful base for noodle soups, dipping sauces or one-pot noodle dishes. Make a favorite Japanese soup by heating the stock with two to three tablespoons medium miso paste, four ounces diced fresh tofu, one minced green onion and cooked somen noodles.

---

1 (5-inch) piece good-quality dried kelp (dashi konbu)
4-1/2 cups bottled spring water or tap water
1/3 rounded cup dried bonito shavings (katsuo bushi)

Make 3 slits in kelp with a sharp knife. Place kelp and water in a medium-size saucepan over medium heat. Bring just to the boiling point; remove from heat. Add bonito shavings. After 3 minutes strain stock into a medium-size bowl through a very fine strainer. Use at once or refrigerate 2 days. Makes about 4 cups stock.

Variation

Instant Dashi: A quick version of dashi can be made by simmering 1 small envelope dashi-no-moto (instant dashi) with 6 cups water 2 minutes.

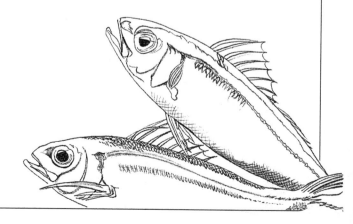

Chicken Stock with Ginger

Flavorful homemade stock is indispensable for making rich satisfying soups or stews. This gingery stock is a good base for Oriental recipes. Increase the stock's flavor-depth and substitute meaty pork bones for the chicken parts. If you are short on time and need stock, improve canned stock by simmering it with chicken parts, green onions and sliced gingerroot 30 minutes.

1 (3-1/2-lb.) chicken, well rinsed
2-1/2 to 3 pounds chicken parts (backs, necks and wings)
6 to 8 green onions or 2 leeks, cut in half, well rinsed and cut into pieces
4 (1/4-inch-thick) slices fresh gingerroot, smashed
About 5 quarts water

Place all ingredients in a stockpot over medium-high heat. When stock bubbles, reduce heat to low. Simmer, uncovered, 30 minutes, skimming off foam from top. Remove breast and thigh meat; reserve for another use. Continue simmering at least 1 hour. Strain stock; discard solids. For greater clarity, strain stock in a strainer lined with cheesecloth. Cool stock; store in the refrigerator up to 3 days. Skim fat off surface. For longer storage, freeze in 1-quart amounts. Makes about 4 quarts.

Variation

Chicken Stock with Herbs: Omit gingerroot. Add the leeks or 2 coarsely chopped medium-size onions. Add 2 celery stalks, 1 carrot, 1 bay leaf, a few black peppercorns and a handful of mixed, fresh herbs such as parsley, thyme and basil.

Miso Ramen

*The Japanese are passionate about ramen. Most often, it is served in
a bowl of soup. Miso ramen is a specialty of Sapporo, capital city of Hokkaido. The
ramen is served in a miso-flavored stock and is often embellished with corn and bean
sprouts. In Northern Japan, a pat of butter is sometimes added to the soup bowl.*

---

1 pound fresh ramen noodles or 12 ounces dried chuka soba
1 teaspoon sesame oil
1 tablespoon vegetable oil
2 green onions, thinly sliced
1 garlic clove, minced
1-1/2 teaspoons minced gingerroot
4 cups Chicken Stock with Ginger (page 24) or Dashi (page 23)
3 tablespoons red miso paste
2 tablespoons water
Seven-Spice Powder (page 13)

In a large pot, bring 3 quarts water to a boil; add noodles. Cook 30 seconds. Cook dried noodles 2 minutes. Drain; rinse under warm water to remove starch. Drain again. Coat with sesame oil. Heat a medium-size saucepan over medium-high heat; add vegetable oil. Cook green onions, garlic and gingerroot 30 seconds; pour in stock. In a small bowl, blend miso paste with the 2 tablespoons water. Stir into stock. Reduce heat to low; simmer 1 or 2 minutes. Divide noodles among deep soup bowls. Ladle stock over noodles. Season with spice mixture. Makes 4 to 6 servings.

Variation

For a slightly thickened soup stock, blend 1 teaspoon cornstarch with 2 tablespoons water; stir into simmering soup.

Copper Well Street Noodles

Throughout China, noodle snacks can be purchased from street hawkers. In Chengdu, capital of Szechuan Province, the Tung Ching or Copper Well Street Noodle Shop is famous for its hot and spicy noodles. The shop began selling noodles in the streets from handcarts about 75 years ago. This spicy noodle recipe is similar to Tung Ching noodles and would make excellent picnic fare.

Sesame Sauce, see below
1 recipe Chinese Egg Noodles (page 8) or 8 ounces fresh ramen
2 green onions, minced
1 small cucumber, seeded, cut into matchstick strips

Sesame Sauce:

1/2 cup toasted sesame seeds
1 large garlic clove
3 tablespoons soy sauce
2 tablespoons Chinese red vinegar or rice vinegar
1-1/2 tablespoons light brown sugar
1/2 teaspoon salt
Dash of ground Szechuan peppercorns
1 teaspoon vegetable oil
2 to 3 teaspoons hot chile oil or hot pepper sauce

Prepare Sesame Sauce. In a large pot, bring 3 quarts water to a boil; add noodles. Cook 1 minute or until tender yet firm to the bite. Drain well. Rinse under cool water. Drain again. Place into a large bowl. Mix in Sesame Sauce and green onions. Divide noodles among serving bowls. Sprinkle each portion with cucumber. Makes 4 servings.

Sesame Sauce

In a Japanese grinding bowl or a blender, grind sesame seed, garlic and soy sauce to a paste. Blend in remaining ingredients until sauce is smooth. Makes about 1/2 cup.

Indonesian Chicken Stew with Rice Sticks

Soto Ayem is a delicious stew with a peppery bite from fiery small chiles.
You can embellish the basic soup recipe by adding two or three additional ingredients
such as hard-cooked egg quarters, chopped shrimp, shredded chicken, fried tofu cubes,
crispy fried onions, fresh bean sprouts or julienne carrots.

2 tablespoons vegetable oil
1 stalk fresh lemongrass or 1 teaspoon freshly grated lemon zest
2 large garlic cloves, smashed
4 large shallots, smashed
2 gingerroot slices, smashed
1/2 teaspoon ground turmeric
1 teaspoon whole black peppercorns
2-1/2 quarts Chicken Stock with Ginger (page 24)
Salt to taste
2 ounces (1/8-inch-wide) rice sticks, soaked in warm water 10 minutes
1 or 2 tiny fresh red chiles, seeded, thinly sliced
3 green onions, thinly sliced
1/4 cup shredded fresh cilantro
4 limes, cut into wedges

Heat oil in a large saucepan over medium heat. Add lemongrass, garlic, shallots, gingerroot, turmeric and peppercorns. Stir 1 minute or until aromatic. Add stock. Cover pan; simmer 20 minutes. Strain stock; return to pan. Add salt. Drain rice sticks. In a medium-size pot, bring 2 quarts water to a boil; add rice sticks. Cook 2 to 3 minutes or until tender yet firm to the bite. Drain and rinse with cool water. Drain again; press out excess water. Add chiles, onions and cilantro to soup. Divide noodles among 6 large shallow bowls. Fill bowls with hot soup. Serve with lime wedges. Makes 6 servings.

Sparerib Soup with Ramen

Soki soba is one of the soups I enjoyed most in Okinawa, Japan. A specialty at soba shops, soki soba is made with ramen. Along with a huge bowl of soup, you are given a small empty dish to hold the sparerib bones. I have simplified matters by removing the bones from the meat before the soup is served.

3 quarts Chicken Stock with Ginger (page 24)
5 green onions, smashed
1 garlic clove, smashed
2 dried shiitake mushrooms
1 pound pork baby back ribs, cut into single ribs
1 small carrot, cut into matchstick strips
1 cup torn Swiss chard or spinach
1/4 cup soy sauce
1/4 teaspoon pepper
Salt to taste
8 ounces fresh ramen noodles or 6 ounces dried Chinese noodles
1 teaspoon sesame oil
2 green onions, minced
Seven-Spice Powder (page 13)
Takuan (pickled yellow daikon radish)

In a large stockpot, bring stock, 3 green onions, garlic and mushrooms to a boil. Reduce heat. In a large pot, blanch ribs in boiling water 1 minute. Drain ribs; add to stock. Cover and simmer 1-1/2 hours or until meat is tender. Remove ribs from soup. Strain stock into a large pan; add back to stockpot. Skim off excess fat. Remove meat from bones; add meat to the pot. Add carrot, Swiss chard, soy sauce, salt and pepper. Simmer on low heat. In a large pot, bring 3 quarts water to a boil; add noodles. Cook 30 seconds. Cook dried noodles 2 minutes. Drain; rinse under warm water to remove starch. Drain again. Divide among 6 large soup bowls. Stir in sesame oil and ladle hot soup mixture over noodles. Garnish soup with minced green onions. Season with Seven-Spice Powder. Serve small dishes of takuan on the side. Makes 6 servings.

Afghan Noodle Soup with Meatballs, Yogurt & Mint

Afghanistan is a land of contrasts; scorching parched deserts, cold mountain ranges, subtropical valleys and plains. Generous hospitality is part of the Afghan code of honor. Aush is a popular noodle soup which doubles as a time-tested remedy for colds. The secret must be the addition of a double dose of hot red pepper and garlic which is believed to initiate a speedy cure.

1 medium-size onion
8 ounces ground lamb or lean ground beef
2 tablespoons chopped fresh parsley
1/2 teaspoon ground cumin
1 egg yolk
1/4 teaspoon ground black pepper
1 tablespoon vegetable oil
2 large garlic cloves, minced
1 cup peeled, chopped tomatoes
3 cups Chicken Stock with Herbs (page 24) made with fresh parsley
4 ounces fresh linguini, fettuccine or tagliatelle or 2 ounces dried noodles
1/2 teaspoon salt, or to taste
1/4 teaspoon ground red (cayenne) pepper, or to taste
2 tablespoons chopped fresh mint
1/2 cup plain yogurt

With a sharp knife, chop onion. Mince 2 tablespoons of the onion; place in a medium-size bowl. Reserve remaining chopped onion. To the bowl of minced onion, add lamb, parsley, cumin, egg yolk and black pepper. Mix ingredients together. Shape into meatballs, using 1 tablespoon meat mixture per meatball. Set aside. In a medium-size saucepan, heat oil. Add reserved onion and garlic and sauté 2 minutes. Add tomatoes and stock. Place meatballs in the tomato mixture. Cover pan; simmer on low heat 5 minutes or until meatballs are cooked through. In a large pot, bring 3 quarts water to a boil; add linguini. Cook 1 minute or until noodles are tender yet firm to the bite. Cook dried noodles slightly longer. Drain noodles; add to meatballs and stock. Stir in salt, cayenne and mint. Serve hot soup in large bowls. Stir 1 to 2 tablespoons yogurt into each serving just before eating. Makes 4 servings.

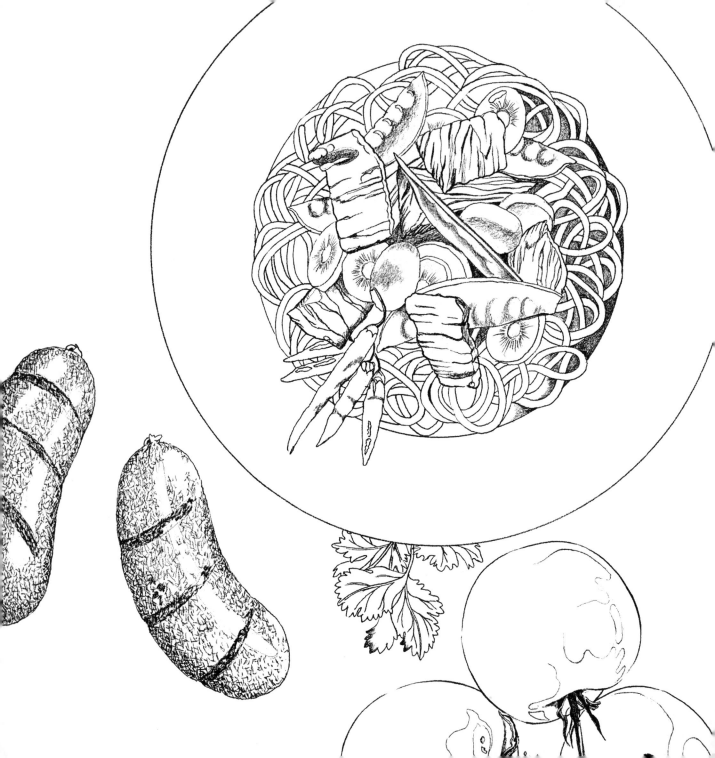

Noodles with Meat

If you love thick juicy steaks but know you need to cut down your meat consumption in an effort to streamline your diet, take a tip from the chefs of Asia. In Asia, unlike in the West, meat is a costly commodity and is consumed in small portions. A small portion of meat can be stretched with healthy fillers such as vegetables and noodles to create an endless variety of dishes.

To accomplish this feat, the meat is sliced into small pieces, then soaked in a highly seasoned marinade. The marinade adds a unique flavor and it will tenderize less tender cuts of meat. Meats should be marinated at least six hours or as long as overnight. Do not marinate longer than 24 hours or the meat fibers will break down making the meat "mushy."

The Chinese have devised numerous ways to prepare meats such as stir-frying, grilling, deep-frying and braising. Stir-frying is a rapid cooking technique which helps lock in meat flavor and moisture. One of my favorite stir-fry dishes is Pan-fried Crispy Noodles with Beef (page 40). The stir-fried saucy beef and vegetable mixture is poured over a crispy noodle cake, which is really the highlight of the meal. Popular in Southern China, the noodle cake is a delicious snack even without the stir-fry, with just a spicy bottled condiment topping.

Pork, the favored meat of China, is appreciated for its sweet, succulent taste. Chinese Roast Pork (page 42) is a prized recipe in which pork tenderloin is marinated, then grilled until crispy brown on the outside and meltingly tender inside. The sliced pork can be added to noodle soups or used to make Roast Pork Lo Mein (page 42).

The Japanese dish Haiyashi Noodles (page 33) has a strong Western influence. Tender steak is cut into strips, cooked with a delicious sauce with vegetables and served over noodles. The steak needs no marination because it is tender. Foods are not seasoned as highly in Japan as in other parts of Asia. But as in China, the real emphasis is on the starch and vegetables, rather than the meat.

Europeans take pasta quite seriously, especially the Italians. The casual Southern Italian dish, Layered Spaghetti with Pancetta, Fontina & Fresh Herbs (page 38) adds an element of fun to dining and will please even the most devoted noodle fans. Pancetta is a form of bacon, but unsmoked. You can substitute prosciutto, blanched bacon or even your favorite ham.

Braised Szechuan Pork Roast over Chinese Noodles

This braised pot roast has a special Oriental flavor. It is cooked slowly and seasoned with gingerroot, soy sauce and a spicy sauce. Leftover meat can be added to noodle soups or stir-fried noodle dishes. If you decide to use beef, substitute beef stock for the chicken stock called for in the recipe.

1 tablespoon vegetable oil
3-1/2 pounds boneless pork shoulder roast or beef chuck roast
5 green onions
2 garlic cloves, minced
1 tablespoon minced fresh gingerroot
6 cups chicken stock, beef stock or water
2 tablespoons soy sauce
1/2 cup San-J Hot & Spicy Szechuan All-Purpose Sauce®
1 recipe Chinese Egg Noodles (page 8) or 8 ounces medium-size egg noodles

Heat oil in a medium-size saucepan over medium-high heat. Add pork and sauté on all sides. Slice 3 green onions into 1-inch lengths. Add to meat with garlic and gingerroot; cook 1 minute. Add stock, soy sauce and spicy sauce. Cover pan; simmer 1-1/2 hours or until tender. Drain off fat, if desired. Slice meat into serving pieces. In a large pot, bring 3 quarts water to a boil; add noodles. Cook fresh noodles 1 to 2 minutes or until tender yet firm to the bite. Cook dried noodles 5 to 6 minutes. Drain well. Divide among large noodle bowls. Top with portions of meat and gravy. Mince remaining green onions; scatter over meat and noodles. Makes 4 to 6 servings.

Note

If San-J Hot & Spicy Szechuan All-Purpose Sauce® is not available, substitute 1/3 cup Tonkatsu Sauce® and 2 to 3 tablespoons hot chile paste with garlic.

Haiyashi Noodles

This Japanese dish has a strong Western influence. The savory steak and mushroom sauce is served over rice or noodles. This recipe was shared with us by the father of our exchange student, a restaurateur in Tokyo. It is one of his favorite dishes to make at home. In Japan, the sauce might contain less meat and more vegetables.

8 ounces tender beef steak, thinly sliced, cut into 2-inch by 1/8-inch pieces
1 tablespoon soy sauce
Freshly ground pepper
2 tablespoons vegetable oil
3 tablespoons butter
1 medium-size onion, cut in half, thinly sliced
4 ounces fresh shiitake mushrooms or button mushrooms, stemmed, sliced
1 large garlic clove, minced
2 tablespoons all-purpose flour
1 cup beef stock or tomato stock
1 carrot, thinly sliced on the diagonal, blanched 1 minute
1/4 cup green peas
2 tablespoons Japanese tonkatsu sauce or 1 tablespoon Worcestershire sauce
12 ounces whole-wheat or plain pappardelle or other wide egg noodles

In a medium-size bowl, season beef with soy sauce and pepper. Heat 1 tablespoon of the oil in a medium-size skillet over medium-high heat. Add beef and sauté. Add remaining tablespoon oil and 1 tablespoon of the butter. Add onion and sauté 4 minutes. Add mushrooms; cook 2 to 3 minutes. Add garlic; cook 30 seconds. Remove vegetables; add to meat. Melt remaining butter in skillet. Stir in flour; stir 3 to 4 minutes or until medium-brown. Whisk in stock; cook 2 minutes. Return meat and vegetables to skillet. Stir in carrot, peas and tonkatsu sauce. Simmer mixture on low heat 4 or 5 minutes. Taste to correct seasonings. In a large pot, bring 3 quarts water to a boil; add noodles. Cook 3 to 4 minutes or until tender yet firm to the bite. Drain noodles; divide among serving plates. Spoon meat and sauce over noodles. Makes 3 or 4 servings.

Tagliatelle with Beef Tenderloin, Shiitake Mushrooms & Sun-dried Tomatoes

Tagliatelle and fettuccine are similar flat ribbon noodles. They are interchangeable in recipes. Homemade tagliatelle is popular in Bologna in the Emilia-Romagna region; fettuccine is the Roman name. Basic Egg Noodles are like tagliatelle. This dish would also be nice made with tomato or herb pasta.

8 ounces beef tenderloin, cut into thin strips
Salt and pepper to taste
2 tablespoons olive oil
2 tablespoons butter
8 ounces fresh shiitake mushrooms or button mushrooms, stemmed, sliced
2 shallots, minced
2 garlic cloves, finely minced
2 ounces sun-dried tomatoes, rehydrated, cut into thin strips (about 1 cup)
1/2 cup chicken stock
1/2 cup oiled-packed ripe olives, pitted, sliced
2 tablespoons chopped fresh basil leaves
1 tablespoon chopped fresh Italian parsley
1 recipe Basic Egg Noodles (page 6) or 8 to 9 ounces fresh fettuccine

In a medium-size bowl, season beef with salt and pepper. In a large skillet, heat 1 tablespoon oil and 1 tablespoon butter over medium-high heat. Add beef and sauté 1 minute or until no longer pink. Remove to a platter. Add remaining oil and butter. Add mushrooms, shallots and garlic and sauté 30 seconds. Stir in tomatoes and chicken stock. Cook 2 to 3 minutes. Add beef, olives and herbs to skillet. Stir to combine ingredients. Reduce heat; keep warm. In a large pot, bring 3 quarts water to a boil; add noodles. Cook 2 to 3 minutes or until tender yet firm to the bite. Drain well. Add to skillet; toss to combine ingredients. Season with additional salt and pepper, if desired. Makes 4 servings.

Korean Noodle Bowl with Marinated Grilled Beef

Bean sprouts, spinach, cabbage or carrot strips would make colorful additions to the stir-fried meat mixture. Serve each bowl of noodles with a side dish of spicy kim chee or pickled cucumbers. Kochu jang is a sweet-hot Korean bean paste.

2 tablespoons soy sauce
1 tablespoon dry white wine
2 tablespoons Korean hot bean paste (kochu jang)
3 garlic cloves, minced
1 teaspoon minced gingerroot
1 tablespoon sugar
1/4 teaspoon black pepper
12 ounces beef rib-eye or other tender beef, partially frozen, sliced 1/8 inch thick
12 ounces dried Korean wheat noodles, Chinese egg noodles or spaghettini
1 tablespoon sesame oil
3 tablespoons vegetable oil
4 green onions, shredded diagonally
1 large red bell pepper, cut into julienne strips
1 tablespoon toasted sesame seeds

In a medium-size bowl, combine soy sauce, wine, bean paste, garlic, gingerroot, sugar and black pepper. Add meat; marinate 30 minutes. In a large pot, bring 3 quarts water to a boil; add noodles. Cook 3 to 4 minutes or until tender yet still firm to the bite. Drain well; rinse under cool water. Drain again. Coat with sesame oil. Divide noodles among 4 large noodle bowls; set aside. Heat a wok or large skillet over high heat. When hot, add 1 tablespoon vegetable oil. Stir-fry green onions and bell pepper 1 minute; remove from pan. Add remaining oil. Stir-fry meat 1 to 2 minutes or until done; mix in vegetables. Top each noodle bowl with 1/4 of the meat mixture. Sprinkle with sesame seeds. Makes 4 servings.

Afghan Green Onion Dumplings with Meat Sauce & Yogurt

This is a famous pasta dish called "aushak" from Afghanistan. Scholars believe dumplings originated somewhere along the silk route from the Far East to Italy. Savory lamb sauce is spooned over emerald dumplings, then topped with a dollop of garlicky yogurt sauce. Chinese chives are the traditional filling, but minced green onions or leeks work well.

Yogurt Sauce, see below
1 cup packed minced green onions, green ends only (use white parts in Meat Sauce)
1/4 teaspoon salt
1 tablespoon vegetable oil
Meat Sauce, see below
1 (1-lb.) package fresh won-ton wrappers (about 60 wrappers)
2 tablespoons chicken bouillon granules

Yogurt Sauce:

1 cup plain yogurt
1/4 cup dairy sour cream
1 large garlic clove, minced
1 tablespoon minced fresh mint or 1 tablespoon dried leaf mint

Meat Sauce:

1 tablespoon vegetable oil
1 cup minced green onions, white parts reserved from dumplings
3 large garlic cloves, minced
1 pound lean ground lamb or beef
4 medium-size tomatoes, seeded, chopped
1 cup tomato sauce
1 teaspoon paprika
1 teaspoon sugar
1 teaspoon salt
1/4 teaspoon pepper
Dash of ground cinnamon

Prepare Yogurt Sauce. In a small bowl, combine green onions, salt and oil; set aside. Prepare Meat Sauce. While sauce is cooking, pour off excess liquid from onion filling mixture. Place 1 teaspoon onion filling in the middle of a won-ton wrapper. Rub edges lightly with water; place another won-ton wrapper on top. Press edges tightly to seal. With a round 3-inch metal cutter, cut dumpling into a circular shape. Or trim with a pair of pinking scissors. With the tines of a fork, press around the sealed edge to make a fluted design. Place dumpling on a lightly oiled tray; cover lightly with plastic wrap to prevent drying. Prepare remaining dumpling; place in a single layer. In a large pot, bring 3 quarts water and the bouillon granules to a boil. Add half of the dumplings to the broth; reduce heat and simmer 1 to 2 minutes. Dumplings will float when done. With a slotted spoon, remove to a large oiled platter; keep warm. Cook remaining dumplings. Divide dumplings among serving plates. Spoon Meat Sauce over each portion. Top with a spoonful of Yogurt Sauce. Makes 4 or 5 main-dish servings or 8 to 10 appetizer servings.

Yogurt Sauce

In a medium-size bowl, combine all ingredients. Makes 1-1/4 cups.

Meat Sauce

Heat oil in a medium-size saucepan over medium-low heat. Add onions and garlic and sauté until soft. Add meat; cook until no longer pink. Add remaining ingredients. Reduce heat to low. Cover pan; simmer 30 minutes, stirring several times.

Variation

For a unique first-course, prepare half of the recipe for Basic Egg Noodles (page 6). Cut into 5-inch squares. Boil until al dente. For each serving, arrange 1 noodle on a plate; spoon Meat Sauce and Yogurt Sauce on top. Makes 8 servings.

Layered Spaghetti with Pancetta, Fontina & Fresh Herbs

This recipe came from my sister Dee Bradney who lived in Naples, Italy with her family for several years. Sometimes, she adds sautéed fresh mushrooms or sun-dried tomato strips to the filling. Salt-cured pancetta resembles bacon, but isn't smoked. If pancetta is unavailable, substitute six slices of blanched bacon. Homemade tomato sauce can be served over each serving.

1 tablespoon each shredded fresh Italian parsley, basil and oregano

3 large eggs

6 tablespoons freshly grated Parmesan cheese

4 green onions, thinly sliced

2 garlic cloves, minced

1/2 teaspoon salt

1/4 teaspoon freshly ground pepper

8 ounces spaghettini

1/4 cup olive oil

5 to 6 ounces fontina cheese, Bel Paese cheese or mozzarella cheese, cut into thin slices

4 ounces pancetta, sliced, cut into pieces, sautéed until crisp

In a large bowl, combine herbs, eggs, Parmesan cheese, onions, garlic, salt and pepper; set aside. Bring a large pot of water to a boil; add salt and spaghettini. Cook 4 to 6 minutes or until tender yet firm to the bite. Drain well; rinse under cool water. Drain again. Stir into cheese mixture. Heat a nonstick 10-inch skillet over medium-high heat. Add 2 tablespoons of the oil. When hot, spread half the pasta mixture over skillet. Layer sliced cheese and pancetta on top. Cover with remaining mixture. Cook 4 minutes, shaking pan often or until the bottom is golden-brown and crispy. Place a large serving plate over the skillet; invert spaghettini noodles onto a platter. Reheat skillet; add remaining oil. Carefully slide spaghettini noodles back into skillet. Cook 4 minutes or until golden-brown and cheese melts. Slide onto a warm serving platter. Makes 4 generous main-dish servings or 8 side-dish servings.

Tagliatelle with Green Beans, Ham & Mushrooms

Ribbonlike tagliatelle is combined with ham and fresh vegetables into a colorful one-dish meal. Partially cooked in the microwave, the beans only need last-minute heating in the skillet. They will retain their bright color, flavor and nutrients.

3 tablespoons butter
8 ounces mushrooms, sliced
1 large garlic clove, minced
8 ounces fresh green beans, trimmed, cut in half, precooked until crisp-tender
6 ounces baked ham, cut into julienne strips
1 recipe Basic Egg Noodles (page 6) or 8 to 9 ounces fresh fettuccine or linguini
1/4 cup freshly grated Parmesan cheese
2 tablespoons chopped fresh basil leaves
1/3 cup whipping cream
Salt and freshly ground pepper to taste

In a large skillet, melt butter over medium-high heat. Add mushrooms and sauté 3 minutes or just until tender. Stir in garlic; cook 30 seconds. Mix in green beans and ham; cook 1 minute. Keep warm. Bring 3 quarts water to a boil in a large pot; add noodles. Cook 1 to 2 minutes or until tender yet firm to the bite. Drain well; add to the skillet. Stir in cheese, basil, cream, salt and pepper. Cook 1 minute, stirring to combine ingredients, until warm. Makes 2 or 3 main-dish servings or 4 side-dish servings.

Note

To precook beans: Spread beans on an ovenproof plate; sprinkle with water. Cover with plastic wrap. Microwave on full power (HIGH) 4 to 4-1/2 minutes. This can be done 1 or 2 hours ahead.

Pan-fried Crispy Noodles with Beef

Topped with a saucy meat and vegetable stir-fry, this crispy-fried noodle cake is sure to be a big hit! Long marination tenderizes the meat and adds succulent flavor. Shredded pork can be substituted for the beef.

Marinade, see below
8 to 12 ounces beef chuck roast or flank steak, partially frozen, cut into paper-thin strips, about 1-1/2 inches long
Spicy Sauce, see below
1 recipe Chinese Egg Noodles (page 8) or 8 ounces dried Chinese egg noodles
8 tablespoons vegetable oil
1 medium-size onion, cut in half, thinly sliced
1 carrot, scraped, thinly sliced on the diagonal
1 red bell pepper, cut into thin strips
2 garlic cloves, minced
2 cups napa cabbage or baby bok choy, cut into 1-1/2-inch pieces
2 green onions, minced

Marinade:

2 tablespoons soy sauce
1 tablespoon dry white wine
1 teaspoon cornstarch
1/8 teaspoon freshly ground pepper
1 teaspoon sesame oil

Spicy Sauce:

1 cup chicken stock or water
1 tablespoon soy sauce
2 tablespoons oyster sauce or brown bean sauce
2 teaspoons hot chile sauce with garlic, or to taste
4 teaspoons cornstarch

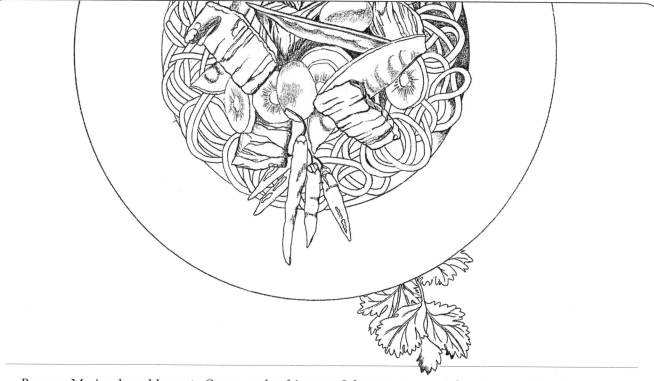

Prepare Marinade; add meat. Cover and refrigerate 8 hours or overnight. Prepare Spicy Sauce; set aside. In a large pot, bring 3 quarts water to a boil; add noodles. Cook 1 minute or until tender yet firm to the bite. Cook dried noodles several minutes longer. Do not overcook; noodles will be cooked again. Drain well; rinse under cool water. Drain again. Coat with 1 tablespoon of the oil. Heat a non-stick 12-inch skillet. Add 2 tablespoons of the oil. Spread noodle mixture over skillet. Cook 4 to 5 minutes, shaking pan often, until golden-brown and crispy. Place a large serving plate over the skillet; invert noodles onto platter. Reheat skillet; add 2 tablespoons of the oil. Carefully slide noodle cake back into skillet. Cook 2 to 3 minutes or until the bottom is light golden-brown. As noodles cook, heat a wok or large skillet. Add 2 tablespoons of the oil. Add meat; stir-fry 1 minute. Remove to a platter. Add remaining 1 tablespoon oil. Add onion, carrot, bell pepper and garlic. Stir-fry 2 minutes. Add cabbage. Stir Spicy Sauce; pour into wok. Stir until mixture thickens and cabbage wilts. Stir meat into mixture. Slide noodles onto a large platter. Pour meat mixture on top of noodles. Top with green onions. Serve at once. Makes 3 or 4 servings.

Marinade

In a medium-size bowl, combine all ingredients.

Spicy Sauce

In a small bowl, combine all ingredients.

Chinese Roast Pork Lo Mein

In Cantonese, "lo" means tossed and "mein" means noodle. If you see a dish on a menu with the words lo-mein, the noodles have been tossed with a variety of stir-fried ingredients. Add the sliced roast pork in this recipe to noodle soups or cold noodle dishes. For spicy noodles, stir in 1 tablespoon of your favorite brand of Oriental hot sauce.

8 ounces Chinese Roast Pork (see below)
8 ounces Chinese egg noodles or 1 recipe Chinese Egg Noodles (page 8)
4 tablespoons vegetable oil
1 small onion, cut in half, thinly sliced
2 teaspoons minced gingerroot
4 stalks bok choy, halved lengthwise, diagonally sliced
2 garlic cloves, minced
4 ounces medium-size shrimp, cooked, cleaned, cut into chunks
1 tablespoon oyster sauce
1 green onion, minced
1-1/2 tablespoons soy sauce, or to taste

Chinese Roast Pork:

1 heaping tablespoon hoisin sauce
2 tablespoons soy sauce
2 tablespoons honey
1/8 teaspoon five-spice powder
1 garlic clove, minced
1 pound pork tenderloin

Prepare Chinese Roast Pork; cut into thin strips. In a large pot, bring 3 quarts water to a boil; add noodles. Cook 1 to 2 minutes or until tender yet firm to the bite. Do not overcook; noodles will be cooked again. Drain well; rinse under cool water. Drain again. Coat with 1 tablespoon of the oil. In a wok or large skillet, heat remaining oil over high heat. Stir-fry onion, gingerroot, cabbage and garlic 3 to 4 minutes. Add shrimp; stir-fry 1 minute. Add pork; stir-fry 1 minute more. Reduce heat. Stir in oyster sauce, noodles and green onion. Season with soy sauce. Makes 2 or 3 main-dish servings.

Chinese Roast Pork

In a small bowl, combine all ingredients except pork. Add pork; turn to coat in mixture. Marinate at least 2 hours or up to 8 hours. Preheat oven to 400°F (205°C). Place meat on a rack inside a foil-lined roasting pan. Cook until meat reaches 165°F (75°C) on a meat thermometer. Cool meat. Slice and use as desired. Refrigerate if not using immediately. Meat can be prepared 1 or 2 days in advance.

Grilled Italian Sausages & Bell Peppers with Eggplant & Fettuccine

Thin, small Oriental eggplants are sweeter than the larger kind. Their thin skins eliminate the need for peeling. Always select eggplants with a firm, shiny skin with no wrinkles. Eggplant is a favorite vegetable in Sicilian cooking.

3 (4-oz.) purple Oriental eggplants, or 1 (12-oz.) eggplant
5 tablespoons extra-virgin olive oil
1 large red onion, cut in half, thinly sliced
3 garlic cloves, minced
2 tablespoons each minced fresh parsley and basil
2 medium-size red bell peppers
2-1/2 to 3 pounds hot or sweet Italian sausages
8 to 9 ounces tomato fettuccine or plain fettuccine
1/4 cup pitted, oil-cured ripe olives, sliced
1/2 cup freshly grated Parmesan cheese

Cut eggplants in half lengthwise, then crosswise into 1/4-inch pieces. In a large skillet over medium-high heat, heat 3 tablespoons of the oil. When oil is hot, add eggplant pieces and sauté until tender. Remove to a platter. Reduce heat to medium. Add remaining 2 tablespoons oil to hot skillet. Add onion and garlic and cook 4 minutes or until soft. Mix in eggplant and herbs; set aside. Preheat grill. Place bell peppers and sausages on hot grill. Grill peppers until the skins have blackened and blistered. Wrap in a clean kitchen towel 5 minutes. Peel off skins. Cut in half. Remove seeds; cut into strips. Add to eggplant. Cook sausages 10 minutes or until cooked through and browned. Keep warm. In a large pot, bring 3 quarts water to a boil; add fettuccine. Cook 1 to 2 minutes or until tender yet firm to the bite. Drain well. Toss with vegetable mixture. Divide fettuccine and sausages among plates. Sprinkle with olives and cheese. Makes 4 servings.

Car Park Noodles

Singapore is a culinary Disneyland. The Orchard Car Park serves as a busy parking lot by day, and a thriving food festival by night. Rice noodle dishes are a specialty at many of the portable food stalls. Fresh rice noodles have a chewy, satisfying texture unlike any other Asian noodle.

Spicy Broth, see below
12 ounces tender beef steak (sirloin or tenderloin)
1-1/2 tablespoons soy sauce
1 tablespoon plus 1 teaspoon cornstarch
4 tablespoons vegetable oil
3 cloves garlic, minced
8 ounces fresh rice noodles or 1 recipe Homemade Rice Noodles (page 3) cut into
 1/2-inch-wide strips
8 ounces baby bok choy, blanched 30 seconds, drained
1/4 cup chopped cilantro

Spicy Broth:

3 cups chicken stock
2 (1/8-inch-thick) slices gingerroot, smashed
1/8 teaspoon five-spice powder
1 tablespoon brown sugar
2 tablespoons soy sauce
1 tablespoon hot chile sauce
2 green onions, sliced
1 tablespoon cornstarch
1 teaspoon sesame oil

Prepare Spicy Broth. Combine beef, soy sauce and the 1 teaspoon cornstarch in a medium-size bowl; set aside. Heat a wok or large skillet over medium-high heat. Add 2 tablespoons of the oil. Stir-fry garlic 30 seconds; add noodles. Stir-fry 1 to 2 minutes. Scoop noodles onto a heated platter. In a small bowl, blend remaining 1 tablespoon cornstarch with 2 tablespoons water. Reheat wok; add remaining oil. Stir-fry meat 1 minute. Pour stock into wok. Add cornstarch mixture; stir-fry 1 minute or until thickened. Stir in bok choy. Pour mixture over noodles. Sprinkle with cilantro. Makes 3 or 4 servings.

Spicy Broth

In a medium-size saucepan, simmer all ingredients except cornstarch and sesame oil 15 minutes or until stock reduces by half. Strain broth. Place back into pan; bring to a boil. Blend cornstarch with 1 tablespoon water. Add to stock; stir 1 minute or until thickened. Add sesame oil. Makes about 1-1/2 cups.

Noodles with Poultry

Your introduction to noodles with chicken may have come in a bowl of chicken-noodle soup when you were a young child. Somewhere deep within that bowl lay limp, soggy noodles and small flecks of chicken. Your main focus was probably on getting a grip on those slippery noodles rather than any special fondness for their flavor. As grown-ups, we still hold a special affinity for chicken and noodle dishes.

Chicken and noodles are a winning combination around the world. Throughout Asia's history, chicken has been a luxury food, appreciated and prepared as often as economically possible. Inexpensive noodles often formed the bulk of an Asian meal. What better way to extend chicken than to combine it with noodles.

Golden Egg Noodles with Spicy Cuban Chicken & Red Peppers (page 53) combines Cuban culinary traditions with chicken and noodles. Although not a traditional starch in Cuban cuisine like beans and rice, the adaptable noodle proves again that it is versatile and international.

Turkey is quick cooking, versatile and nutritious. With great success I have substituted lean ground turkey for pork in the Chinese noodle dish, Szechuan-Style Spaghetti (page 54). The mild flavor of ground turkey blends beautifully with the spicy Oriental seasonings. Turkey is no longer seasonal. It is possible to buy turkey wings, turkey legs and turkey breasts, making good substitutes in your chicken-noodle recipes.

Poultry and noodle dishes are economical, easy to prepare and perfect for entertaining. Their flavors are basic, but you can change their taste and guise with a variety of exciting international seasonings. The possibilities for interesting combinations are limitless. You can "travel around the world" preparing a new dish daily for a year, and still not run out of ideas. My recipes should be a starting point. Let them inspire you to create a collection of new poultry-and-noodle dishes on your own.

Five-Spice Game Hens with Mushroom-Asparagus Lo Mein

Marinated Cornish game hens are grilled and served on a colorful bed of Chinese egg noodles, asparagus, carrots and black mushrooms. You can substitute flavorful dried Oriental mushrooms for the fresh mushrooms. Soften in warm water, then trim off the tough stems. The savory pan drippings will add marvelous flavor to fried noodles.

Five-Spice Marinade, see below
2 Cornish game hens, split in half
2 tablespoons butter, melted
1 recipe Chinese Egg Noodles (page 6) or 8 ounces dried Chinese egg noodles
3 tablespoons vegetable oil
4 green onions, thinly sliced
2 garlic cloves, minced
1 teaspoon grated gingerroot
4 ounces fresh shiitake mushrooms, stems trimmed, sliced
1 pound thin asparagus, cut into 2-inch pieces, blanched 2 minutes
2 carrots, cut into 2-inch julienne strips, blanched 30 seconds
Salt and pepper to taste
1 tablespoon toasted sesame seeds

Five-Spice Marinade:

2 tablespoons hoisin sauce
1 tablespoon dry white wine
1 tablespoon light soy sauce
1 teaspoon chile sauce with garlic
2 teaspoons freshly grated orange peel
1/4 teaspoon five-spice powder
1 teaspoon minced gingerroot
1 tablespoon honey

Prepare Five-Spice Marinade. Coat game hens in mixture. Cover; refrigerate 2 to 6 hours. Preheat oven to 375°F (190°C). Drain off marinade. Place hens, meat-side up, in a roasting pan. Cook until the juices run clear when hens are pierced or a thermometer inserted in the thickest part reads 165°F (75°C). Baste with butter as hens cook. Add a little water to pan if drippings begin to burn. Keep hens warm; remove fat from drippings. Bring 3 quarts water to a boil in a large pot; add noodles. Cook 1

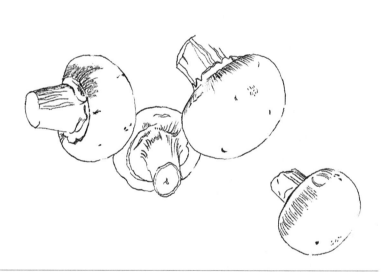

to 2 minutes or until tender yet firm to the bite. Drain well. Rinse under cool water. Drain again. Heat a wok or large skillet over medium heat. Add oil. Add onions, garlic and gingerroot and stir-fry 30 seconds. Add mushrooms; stir-fry 1 minute. Add asparagus and carrot strips. Stir-fry 1 minute or until hot. Reduce heat. Mix in noodles. Season with 2 to 3 tablespoons pan drippings and salt and pepper. Divide noodles among serving plates; top each with 1/2 game hen. Sprinkle with sesame seeds. Makes 4 servings.

Five-Spice Marinade

In a large bowl, combine all ingredients.

Nagasaki Champon

This specialty from Southern Japan could be referred to as chop-suey soup. When you order it in a restaurant you receive a huge bowl of ramen noodles with a mouthwatering thick stew of chicken, pork, seafood and vegetables poured on top. It is representative of a style of cooking called shippoku-ryori, a Japanese version of Chinese cuisine.

2 quarts Chicken Stock with Ginger (page 24)
2 tablespoons dried tree ears, soaked in water 30 minutes, coarsely chopped
3 medium-size dried shiitake mushrooms, soaked in water until soft, stemmed and sliced
3 tablespoons soy sauce
2 ounces pork butt, sliced paper-thin, cut into strips
1 carrot, cut into matchstick strips
2 cups thinly sliced napa cabbage
1/4 cup sliced bamboo shoots
3 tablespoons cornstarch
1/3 cup water
3 ounces sea scallops or kamaboko (fish cake), thinly sliced
1-1/2 cups shredded cooked chicken (reserved from stock)
1 egg, slightly beaten
Salt and freshly ground pepper to taste
12 ounces fresh ramen or yaki soba noodles
2 green onions, thinly sliced
Seven-Spice Powder (page 13)

In a large pot, simmer stock with tree ears, mushrooms and soy sauce 3 minutes. Add pork, carrot, cabbage and bamboo shoots; simmer 2 minutes. Increase heat. Mix cornstarch with 1/3 cup water in a small bowl; stir into pot. Cook 1 minute or until thickened. Reduce heat to low. Add scallops and chicken. Drizzle in egg, stirring in a circular pattern with a pair of chopsticks. Season to taste. Keep warm. Bring 3 quarts water to a boil in a large pot; add noodles. Cook 30 seconds or until tender yet firm to the bite. Drain well. Divide among 6 large soup bowls. Ladle stew on top. Garnish with green onions and Seven-Spice Powder. Makes 6 servings.

Cold-Stirred Noodles with Jade Cilantro Dressing

*Crunchy sesame noodles, Chinese barbecued duck and cilantro dressing
make a magnificent dish which will be a hit at your next luncheon or supper. Without
the duck, the dish is a great side for grilled poultry or steak. Try the
dressing on Japanese wheat noodles or spaghetti and shellfish.*

Jade Cilantro Dressing, see below
1/2 crisp Chinese barbecued duck or barbecued chicken
8 ounces Chinese egg noodles, wheat noodles or ramen
1 tablespoon sesame oil or vegetable oil
1 heaping tablespoon toasted sesame seeds
1/2 carrot, cut into matchstick strips
1 small yellow or red bell pepper, cut into matchstick strips
2 green onions, thinly sliced

Jade Cilantro Dressing:

1/4 cup torn cilantro leaves
1 large garlic clove
1 teaspoon fresh minced gingerroot
2 tablespoons rice vinegar
1 teaspoon Dijon-style mustard
2 teaspoons sugar
1/2 teaspoon salt
1/4 cup safflower oil

Prepare Jade Cilantro Dressing. Remove meat and skin from the duck bones. Trim fat off meat and skin; cut into thin strips. Set aside. (Omit skin, if desired.) In a large pot, bring 3 quarts water to a boil; add noodles. Cook 1 to 2 minutes or until tender yet firm to the bite. Drain well; rinse under cool water. Drain again. Mix with oil and sesame seeds. Toss noodles with carrot strips, bell pepper strips and duck. Add enough dressing to coat mixture; toss to mix. Divide noodles among serving plates; garnish with green onions. Makes 2 or 3 main-dish servings.

Jade Cilantro Dressing

In a blender, puree cilantro, garlic and gingerroot with rice vinegar. Add mustard, sugar and salt. Slowly add oil, beating just until blended. Makes about 1/3 cup.

Japanese Hot Pot with Udon, Chicken & Vegetables

Nabe-yaki udon can be prepared in a large pottery casserole dish (donabe) or individual casserole dishes. If you don't have either, use an electric skillet or wok. Other ingredients you might want to add are spinach, carrots, shrimp, shrimp tempura, crab legs or fried bean curd pouches (abura-age). The noodles are cooked by the shimizu method, which means cold water is periodically added as the noodles cook.

6 cups Chicken Stock with Ginger (page 24) or Dashi (page 23)
2 (1/8-inch-thick) slices gingerroot, smashed
3 tablespoons light soy sauce
2 tablespoons mirin
2 green onions, thinly sliced
8 ounces dried udon or 1 recipe Japanese Udon (page 5)
4 fresh shiitake mushrooms or 4 dried mushrooms, soaked in water until soft
1 whole chicken breast, skinned, boned and thinly sliced
8 thin slices kamaboko (steamed fish cake), cut into 1/4-inch-thick slices
4 or 5 napa cabbage leaves, cut into 2-inch pieces
4 large eggs, if desired
Seven-Spice Powder (page 13)

In a large saucepan, simmer stock with gingerroot 10 minutes. Discard gingerroot. Add soy sauce, mirin and green onions. Keep warm. In a large pot, bring 4 quarts water to a boil; add noodles. Stir noodles; bring to a boil. Pour in 1 cup cold water. Bring back to a boil; add 1 cup cold water. Continue cooking 4 to 5 minutes or until noodles are tender yet slightly firm to the bite. Drain well; rinse under cool water. Place noodles into a large, deep flameproof casserole dish. Arrange remaining ingredients on top. Ladle broth into casserole dish. Simmer over medium heat until chicken and cabbage are cooked. Reduce heat. If eggs are used, crack them on top of stew. Cover; cook until poached. Provide large noodle bowls for diners to eat from. Season with Seven-Spice Powder. Makes 4 servings.

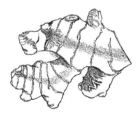

Golden Egg Noodles with Spicy Cuban Chicken & Red Peppers

Chicken and rice are a twosome in Cuba. Here, I have adapted a favorite Cuban recipe and combined it with noodles. We don't think of Cuban foods as fiery-hot, but many Cubans grow chile plants in their backyards. Spicy Oriental hot sauce is especially appropriate since a number of interesting Cuban dishes are seasoned with Oriental spices, thanks to the influx of Chinese workers entering Cuba in the nineteenth century.

---

2 tablespoons extra-virgin olive oil
2 tablespoons butter
1 medium-size onion
2 large garlic cloves, minced
1 teaspoon minced gingerroot
1 large red bell pepper, diced
1 Granny Smith apple, peeled, cored and diced
1-1/2 teaspoons ground coriander
1 rounded teaspoon ground cumin
1/2 teaspoon ground turmeric
1 teaspoon salt, or to taste
1 pound chicken breasts, boned, skinned and cut into 1/2-inch pieces
1 to 2 tablespoons hot chile sauce
1/2 cup plus 2 tablespoons chicken stock
1 teaspoon cornstarch
8 ounces narrow dried egg noodles
1/4 cup minced cilantro

In a heavy medium-size saucepan over medium-low heat, heat olive oil and butter. Add onion, garlic, gingerroot, bell pepper and apple and cook 4 minutes. Stir in coriander, cumin, turmeric and salt; cook 1 minute. Add chicken. Stir gently to coat with spices. Add chile sauce and the 1/2 cup chicken stock. Cover pan; reduce heat and simmer 2 minutes or until chicken is done. In a small bowl, blend remaining stock and cornstarch. Stir into chicken mixture. Cook until thickened. Keep warm. In a large pot, bring 3 quarts water to a boil; add salt and noodles. Cook 5 minutes or until noodles are tender yet firm to the bite. Drain well. Add noodles and cilantro to chicken mixture; toss gently to combine. Makes 4 or 5 servings.

Szechuan-Style Spaghetti

Long uncut noodles are a symbol of good luck and long life in China. This Szechuan dish is popular at Chinese birthday celebrations. Instead of the traditional pork, I have substituted lean ground turkey. Spoon the delicious meat sauce over Chinese Egg Noodles, just like Italian-style spaghetti-and-meat sauce. The crisp, shredded vegetables add a cool, crunchy contrast.

2 tablespoons vegetable oil
3 green onions, minced
2 large garlic cloves, minced
2 teaspoons minced gingerroot
3 dried shiitake mushrooms, soaked in water until soft, stemmed and minced
1 pound ground turkey
1/4 cup finely chopped water chestnuts
2 tablespoons hot bean sauce, brown bean sauce or 1 tablespoon red miso
2 tablespoons hoisin sauce
2 tablespoons soy sauce
1 teaspoon sugar
1/4 teaspoon ground Szechuan pepper
1 teaspoon cornstarch
1 cup chicken stock
1 recipe Chinese Egg Noodles (page 8) or 8 ounces dried Chinese wheat noodles
2 teaspoons sesame oil or vegetable oil
1 cucumber, ends trimmed, seeded, cut into matchstick strips
2 carrots, cut into matchstick strips

Heat a wok or large skillet over high heat. Add oil. Add green onions, garlic, gingerroot and mushrooms and stir-fry 30 seconds. Add turkey; stir-fry 2 minutes or until crumbly. Stir in water chestnuts, bean sauce, hoisin sauce, soy sauce, sugar and Szechuan pepper. Cook 1 minute. Reduce heat slightly. In a small bowl, blend cornstarch and stock. Stir into meat mixture. Stir-fry until mixture thickens. Keep warm. In a large pot, bring 3 quarts water to a boil; add noodles. Cook 1 to 2 minutes or until tender yet firm to the bite. Drain well. Rinse under warm water. Drain again. Coat with sesame oil. Divide noodles among large bowls. Spoon meat mixture on top. Top each portion with shredded cucumber and carrots. Makes 4 or 5 servings.

Turkey Cutlets Chipotle with Red Chile Fettuccine

Chipotle chiles, smoked red jalapeño peppers, add wonderful flavor, aroma and heat to foods. Chipotles have a powerful punch; a little added to a sauce goes a long way. Flattened, boned chicken breasts can be used in this recipe.

1 pound turkey breast cutlets, pounded 1/8 inch thick
1/2 cup all-purpose flour
1/2 teaspoon coarsely ground pepper
3 tablespoons unsalted butter or margarine
2 tablespoons vegetable oil
4 green onions, minced
2 garlic cloves, minced
1/2 teaspoon ground cumin
2 teaspoons chopped fresh oregano or 1 teaspoon dried leaf oregano
1 cup prepared enchilada sauce
1 chipotle chile, or to taste, minced
2 tablespoons whipping cream
1 cup shredded Monterey Jack or provolone cheese
1/4 cup pitted ripe olives, sliced
8 to 9 ounces chile-flavored fettuccine or Chile Tagliatelle (page 6)
2 tablespoons minced cilantro leaves

Preheat oven to 300°F (150°C). Coat cutlets in a mixture of flour and pepper. In a medium-size skillet over medium-high heat, heat 1 tablespoon of the butter and 1 tablespoon of the oil. Add half of cutlets and sauté until golden-brown. Transfer to a large baking dish; keep warm in oven. Repeat with remaining cutlets. To the skillet, add onions, garlic, cumin and oregano; cook 1 minute. Stir in enchilada sauce and chipotle. Cook 1 minute; stir in cream. Top cutlets with sauce and cheese; garnish with olives. Keep warm in the oven. In a large pot, bring 3 quarts water to a boil; add noodles. Cook 1 minute or until tender yet firm to the bite. Drain well. Place in a large bowl; stir in remaining butter and cilantro. Divide among serving plates. Place a cutlet with some sauce on each serving. Makes 4 or 5 servings.

Spaghetti with Chicken Livers, Mushrooms & Rosemary

"Rosemary, that's for remembrance," remarked Shakespeare. If you have a fondness for rosemary and chicken livers, you won't forget this memorable spaghetti dish. Complete the meal with a basket of crisp fresh sliced vegetables and a dipping sauce of herb or Italian dressing. Serve sliced fruits, cheese and nuts for dessert.

2 tablespoons olive oil
2 tablespoons butter
1 large red onion, chopped
8 ounces button mushrooms, sliced
1 tablespoon fresh rosemary or 1 teaspoon dried rosemary
1 cup chicken livers, rinsed, drained and cut into small pieces
1 tablespoon all-purpose flour
2 garlic cloves, minced
1 tablespoon minced fresh parsley
Salt and freshly ground pepper to taste
8 ounces thin spaghetti
1 tablespoon minced fresh chives

Heat 1 tablespoon of the oil and 1 tablespoon of the butter in a large skillet over medium-high heat. Add onion and sauté 2 to 3 minutes. Add mushrooms and rosemary; sauté 4 minutes or until soft. Remove mixture from skillet; set aside. Heat remaining oil and butter in skillet. Mix chicken livers with flour. Add livers to skillet and sauté 4 to 5 minutes or until slightly crispy. Add garlic and parsley; cook 1 minute more. Mix in mushrooms. Keep warm. As livers are cooking, in a large pot bring 3 quarts water to a boil; add salt and spaghetti. Cook 4 to 6 minutes or until tender yet firm to the bite. Drain well. Stir into skillet mixture. Mix in chives, salt and pepper. Makes 2 or 3 servings.

Mexican Vermicelli with Cilantro-Flavored Cream

In Mexico, this is considered a sopa seca or "dry soup." It is a good example of Mexican home cooking. You will find it easy to chop the chicken meat if you use a large Chinese cleaver and a sturdy cutting board. If you like spicy foods, sprinkle in a few hot chile flakes. The topping of Parmesan cheese and cilantro-flavored cream elevates the status of this dish to company fare.

1/2 cup packed fresh cilantro leaves
1 cup dairy sour cream
2 teaspoons fresh lime juice
8 ounces vermicelli, dried in coils
5 tablespoons vegetable oil
1 small red onion, minced
1/2 green bell pepper, diced
2 garlic cloves, minced
1 whole chicken breast, skinned, boned and coarsely chopped
2 teaspoons fresh minced oregano or 1 teaspoon dried leaf oregano
2 small tomatoes, seeded, chopped
About 1-1/2 cups hot chicken stock
Salt and freshly ground pepper to taste
3/4 cup freshly grated Parmesan cheese, or to taste

In a blender, puree cilantro with sour cream. Add lime juice. Refrigerate until needed. In a large bowl, gently crush coils of vermicelli to break apart. Heat 3 tablespoons of the oil in a large skillet over medium heat. Add noodles and fry until golden-brown. Stir and turn constantly; noodles burn easily. Remove from skillet; add remaining oil. Add onion, bell pepper and garlic and sauté 2 to 3 minutes. Add chicken and oregano; cook, stirring, 1 to 2 minutes. Add noodles, tomatoes and stock. Reduce heat; simmer until noodles are tender and liquid is absorbed. Add a little extra stock if necessary. Season with salt and pepper. Serve with Parmesan cheese and cilantro-flavored cream. Makes 3 or 4 servings.

Noodles with Seafood

During the period I lived in Asia, my favorite noodle dishes were those made with fresh fish and seafood. Fish and seafood are the heart of the Asian diet. Their abundance is well-matched by the unlimited methods in which Asian cooks combine them with noodles. Where else could one find matchmaking skills clever enough to forge alliances among foods such as seafood, pork and rice noodles? This unusual partnership has brought out the best qualities in each of them, allowing the creation of dishes such as Thai Fried Rice Noodles with Pork & Shrimp (page 65).

Tokyo Spaghetti (page 60) is a personal favorite which I often encounter in Japanese restaurants throughout America. In my version, grilled salmon is brushed with a rich teriyaki glaze, then served on a bed of aromatic stir-fried noodles.

Create your own interesting seafood-noodle combinations at home. Steamed fish fillets or steaks can be flaked and stirred into cold noodle dishes. Or, small marinated pieces of raw fish or shellfish can be stir-fried, then tossed in the pan with the noodles. The choice of seasoning is yours. When the Chinese cook fish, they like to add ginger and green onions. Korean cooks add garlic, ginger, hot chiles and sesame oil. Filipinos may add fish sauce, ginger, tomato, vinegar, garlic or onion. Vietnamese cooks add lemongrass, shallots, mint and cilantro.

Seafood dishes are easy to prepare, often requiring only last minute cooking. Take a cooking tip from the Oriental experts: marinate your raw fish a few minutes before cooking it with a little sherry, fresh gingerroot and green onion. These three ingredients add wonderful flavor to any kind of fish, and will neutralize mild fishy odors. They are not used with the intention of masking odors of less-than-fresh fish, but to enhance the flavors of fresh fish. There is no substitute for freshness—prized above all else by Asian cooks.

Tokyo Spaghetti

This trendy dish is a favorite at Japanese restaurants in America. Succulent grilled salmon teriyaki is served on a bed of well-seasoned fried noodles. This dish is equally delicious made with shrimp, scallops, chicken or squid teriyaki. The Japanese also love cod roe (tarako). It is usually mixed into the cooked spaghetti.

Ginger-Teriyaki Sauce, see below
1 pound fresh salmon fillets, cut into 2-inch-square pieces
1 tablespoon sake or dry white wine
1 recipe Stir-fried Chinese Noodles with Vegetables (page 72)
1 green onion, minced
Seven-Spice Powder (page 13)

Ginger-Teriyaki Sauce:

1/4 cup soy sauce
1/4 cup mirin
2 tablespoons sake
2 tablespoons sugar
1 (1/8-inch-thick) slice gingerroot
1 tablespoon water
1-1/2 teaspoons cornstarch

Prepare Ginger-Teriyaki Sauce. Place salmon in a shallow pan; add sake. Refrigerate until needed. Soak several bamboo skewers in water. Prepare Stir-Fried Chinese Noodles with Vegetables. Keep warm. Preheat grill. Insert 2 soaked bamboo skewers, running parallel, through each piece of salmon. Grill fish 2 minutes, turning once. Brush both sides with sauce. Grill fish until it barely flakes, 3 to 6 minutes. Do not overcook. Remove from grill; brush liberally with sauce. Divide noodles among serving plates. Remove skewers from fish; portion salmon pieces on top of noodles. Sprinkle with green onion and Seven-Spice Powder. Makes 3 or 4 servings.

Ginger-Teriyaki Sauce

In a small saucepan, combine all ingredients except water and cornstarch. Simmer over medium heat 3 minutes. Blend water with cornstarch; stir into soy sauce mixture. Stir 1 minute or until thickened. Strain sauce. Makes about 1/2 cup.

Noodles with Crabmeat in Peanut Sauce

*This chile-and-peanut-flavored noodle dish can be served as
a light luncheon dish, a hearty snack or as part of a multi-course meal. Meat
lovers might prefer to add one cup slivered ham in place of the seafood.*

Peanut Sauce, see below
1 recipe Chinese Egg Noodles (page 8) or 12 ounces fresh ramen or 8 ounces dried spaghettini
2 teaspoons sesame oil
8 ounces lump crabmeat or cooked baby shrimp
1 small carrot, cut into matchstick strips
2 green onions, minced
3 tablespoons chopped dry-roasted peanuts
1/4 cup packed torn cilantro leaves

Peanut Sauce:

2 tablespoons dry-roasted peanuts
1 garlic clove
1/4 cup vegetable oil
1/4 teaspoon salt
1 to 3 teaspoons hot chile paste with garlic (Lan Chi® brand)
1 tablespoon rice vinegar
1 teaspoon sugar
2 teaspoons soy sauce

Prepare Peanut Sauce; set aside. In a large pot, bring 3 quarts water to a boil; add fresh noodles. Cook 1 minute or until tender yet firm to the bite. Dried noodles will take several minutes longer to cook. Drain noodles; rinse under cool water. Drain again. Place in a large bowl; coat with sesame oil. Add crabmeat and carrot; toss ingredients to mix. Mix Peanut Sauce with noodle mixture. Divide noodles among 4 serving plates. Garnish each serving with green onions, chopped peanuts and cilantro leaves. Makes 4 servings.

Peanut Sauce

In a food processor with the metal blade, place peanuts and garlic; grind to a paste. Add vegetable oil, salt, chile paste, vinegar, sugar and soy sauce. Process 15 seconds. Makes about 1/2 cup.

Lemon-Parsley Tagliatelle with Mussels & Salmon

If you like lemon with your seafood, you will love the zesty lemon-flavored pasta mixed with salmon and mussels. You can make this dish with any other type of lemon- or herb-flavored pasta. Serve the pasta with a mixed green salad on the side.

2 pounds live mussels, debearded, scrubbed under cold running water
1/4 cup butter
1 tablespoon olive oil
8 ounces salmon fillets or steaks, skin, bones removed, cut into bite-size pieces
2 garlic cloves, minced
2 green onions, thinly sliced
1 tablespoon fresh lemon juice
1 recipe Lemon-Parsley Tagliatelle (page 6) or 8 to 9 ounces fresh lemon- or herb-flavored pasta
1/3 cup toasted pine nuts
Lemon slices

Place mussels in a large heavy skillet over medium-high heat. Cover pan; cook 5 to 6 minutes, shaking the pan often. When the mussels open, transfer them to a large bowl. Discard any which do not open. Shell mussels; keep warm. Heat butter and oil in a large heavy skillet over medium heat. Add salmon, garlic and green onions. Cook 2 minutes, stirring gently, or until salmon is opaque. Reduce heat to low; stir in lemon juice and mussels. Keep warm. In a large pot, bring 3 quarts water to a boil; add salt and noodles. When water returns to a rapid boil, cook 1 minute or until noodles are tender yet firm to the bite. Dried pasta will take several minutes longer to cook. Drain well. Place in a large heated bowl. Add seafood mixture; combine gently. Spoon onto warm serving plates; garnish with pine nuts and lemon slices. Makes 4 servings.

Stir-fried Somen with Shrimp & Vegetables

In Japan, somen is eaten in a bowl of water with ice cubes. I learned the method below in Okinawa. The tender noodles are stir-fried, Chinese-style. The dish reflects Okinawa's long history under Chinese rule. Somen is used in vegetarian "shojin ryori," or temple cuisine. Omit the seafood for a vegetarian version. Also, try this recipe with hiyamugi, a slightly thicker noodle.

2 (3-oz.) bundles somen (white wheat noodles)
4 tablespoons vegetable oil
1 small onion, halved, thinly sliced
1 small carrot, shredded
1 garlic clove, finely minced
1 teaspoon minced fresh gingerroot
4 ounces chopped peeled shrimp, sliced bay scallops, or crab or lobster surimi
3 small chikuwa (hollow fish rolls), cut into 1/4-inch rings
10 snow peas, blanched, julienned
1 teaspoon dashi-no-moto (powdered fish stock)
1 to 2 tablespoons soy sauce
1/4 teaspoon salt, or to taste
4 thin green onions, sliced

In a medium-size pot, bring 2 quarts water to a boil; add salt and somen. When water returns to a boil, drain somen in a fine strainer. Do not overcook; noodles will be cooked again. Rinse under cool water. Drain again. Coat with 1 tablespoon oil. In a wok or medium-size skillet, heat remaining oil over medium-high heat. Add onion, carrot, garlic and gingerroot; stir-fry 30 seconds. Add shrimp and chikuwa; stir-fry 1 minute. Add pea pods; stir-fry 30 seconds longer. Add somen. Toss with vegetable mixture. Sprinkle in dashi powder, soy sauce, salt and green onions; mix well. Scoop hot somen mixture onto a serving dish. Makes 4 servings.

Crawfish with Angel Hair Pasta

Just what would Cajun cooking be like without crawfish? These freshwater crustaceans contain a delicious golden fat under the shell, which will give your dish a tremendous flavor boost. Mix the delectable crawfish sauce with your favorite lemon, red pepper or cracked black pepper pasta.

2 tablespoons vegetable oil
2 tablespoons butter
12 ounces peeled crayfish tails, or large peeled shrimp, cut into large pieces
1/2 cup thinly sliced green onions
1/3 cup thinly sliced celery
1/3 cup chopped green bell pepper
2 garlic cloves, minced
1 cup whipping cream
Hot pepper sauce to taste
1 tablespoon each minced fresh parsley and thyme
Salt and freshly ground pepper to taste
8 to 9 ounces angel hair pasta, cappellini or vermicelli

In a large skillet, heat 1 tablespoon of the oil and the butter over medium-high heat. Add crayfish and sauté 2 to 3 minutes. Remove from pan. Add remaining oil. Add onions, celery, bell pepper and garlic and sauté 4 minutes or until tender. Add cream. Reduce heat; simmer 5 minutes or until reduced by 1/3. Add hot pepper sauce, herbs, salt and pepper. Simmer 1 minute. Mix in crawfish with juices. Keep sauce warm. In a large pot, bring 3 quarts water to a boil; add pasta. Cook about 1 minute or until tender yet firm to the bite. Drain well. Toss with sauce. Makes 2 or 3 main-dish or 4 first-course servings.

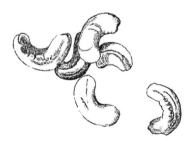

Thai Fried Rice Noodles with Pork & Shrimp

In this noodle dish called Pad Thai you will experience a range of sweet, sour and salty flavors which blend to create the basic Thai taste. The best noodle to use is the 1/8-inch-wide chantaboon rice noodle. To this basic recipe, you can add other ingredients such as fried strips of tofu, salty dried shrimp, carrot slivers, Chinese garlic chives or scrambled egg.

6 ounces dried rice noodles, soaked in warm water 10 minutes
3 tablespoons Southeast Asian fish sauce (page 111)
2 tablespoons water
2 teaspoons sugar
2 tablespoons ketchup
2 tablespoons vegetable oil
6 shallots, thinly sliced
3 large garlic cloves, minced
4 ounces ground pork
8 ounces medium-size shrimp, peeled, cut into 1/2-inch pieces
4 ounces fresh bean sprouts (reserve about 1/4 cup)
3 tablespoons chopped peanuts
3 tablespoons cilantro leaves
1 lime, cut into wedges
Hot chile sauce to taste

Drain noodles. In a large pot, bring 3 quarts water to a boil; add noodles. Cook 3 to 4 minutes or until tender yet still chewy to the bite. Drain and rinse with cool water. Drain again; press out excess water. In a small bowl, combine fish sauce, water, sugar and ketchup. Heat a wok or large skillet over medium-high heat; add vegetable oil. Stir-fry shallots and garlic 2 minutes. Add pork and shrimp; stir-fry 1 minute or until pork is no longer pink. Add bean sprouts and sauce mixture. Reduce heat to low. Mix in noodles. When well mixed, scoop noodles onto a serving platter. Garnish with reserved bean sprouts, peanuts, cilantro and lime wedges. Serve with hot chile sauce; season individual portions as desired. Makes 2 or 3 servings.

Cappellini with Seafood in Saffron-Scented Cream

Golden saffron sauce with seafood coats the extra-thin spaghetti-like noodles called cappellini. For an unforgettable first-course, serve the sauce over black fettuccine. Tinted with squid ink, black pasta is available in many specialty markets. One-half teaspoon toasted black mustard seeds would add an interesting flavor and texture to the sauce.

1/2 cup dry white wine
2 shallots, sliced
1 garlic clove, crushed
2 basil leaves
24 mussels, scrubbed, debearded and rinsed in cold water
2 cups (1 pint) whipping cream
Pinch of saffron threads, if desired
8 ounces medium-size shrimp, cleaned
4 ounces sea scallops, sliced in half
Salt and freshly ground pepper to taste
8 to 9 ounces fresh cappellini or tagliarini or 6 ounces dried noodles
Fresh cilantro leaves

In a large skillet over medium heat, simmer wine, shallots, garlic and basil 1 minute. Add mussels, discarding any that do not close when tapped. Cover pan; cook 4 to 5 minutes, shaking pan often. When mussels open, transfer them to a bowl. Discard any which do not open. Shell mussels; keep warm. Strain broth through a fine sieve or several layers of moistened cheesecloth. Measure 1/2 cup. In a medium-size saucepan over medium heat, simmer cream, broth and saffron threads, if using. Add shrimp and scallops; cook 1 minute. With a slotted spoon, remove seafood from sauce; add to mussels. Cook until cream is reduced to 1-1/2 cups. Stir in shrimp, scallops and mussels. Add salt and pepper. Reduce heat to keep warm. In a large pot, bring 3 quarts water to a boil; add salt and cappellini. Cook noodles 1 to 2 minutes or until tender yet firm to the bite. Dried noodles will take a few minutes longer. Drain well. Place into a large bowl. Add 1/3 of the seafood sauce; combine gently. Divide pasta among plates; spoon remaining sauce on top. Garnish with cilantro. Makes 4 servings.

Filipino Pancit Canton

*"Pancit" is the Filipino word for noodle, representing a wide variety
of popular noodles including pancit bihon, or thin rice vermicelli and pancit sotanghon,
or thin bean threads. Pancit Canton is a fat dried wheat noodle of Chinese origin.
It is cooked, dried, then packaged into large loose bundles.*

---

2 tablespoons dry white wine
8 ounces raw medium-size shrimp, peeled and deveined, or other seafood
1 (8-oz.) package Pancit Canton or chuka soba or 6 ounces vermicelli
5 tablespoons vegetable oil
1 medium-size onion, chopped
2 large garlic cloves, minced
2 teaspoons minced gingerroot
2 cups tender cabbage leaves, cut into 1-inch pieces
1/2 medium-size carrot, cut into matchstick strips
Freshly ground pepper to taste
2 green onions, thinly sliced
1 to 2 tablespoons Southeast Asian fish sauce (page 111)
Salt (optional)

In a medium-size bowl, sprinkle wine over shrimp; set aside. In a large pot, bring 3 quarts water to a boil; add noodles. Cook 2 to 3 minutes or until tender yet firm to the bite. Drain well; rinse under cool water. Drain again. Coat with 1 tablespoon of the vegetable oil. Heat a wok or heavy skillet over high heat. Add 2 tablespoons of the vegetable oil. Drain shrimp; add to wok and stir-fry 1 minute or until they turn pink. Remove shrimp. Wipe wok dry. Reheat wok; add remaining oil. Stir-fry onion, garlic and gingerroot 1 minute. Add cabbage and carrot; stir-fry 2 to 3 minutes. Reduce heat. Mix in noodles and shrimp. Season with pepper, green onions, fish sauce and salt, if desired. Makes 4 or 5 servings.

Shrimp, Sugar Snaps & Oriental Herbs on a Nest of Rice Sticks

This refreshing dish offers a medley of colors, flavors and textures. Fragrant with mint, cilantro and shiso leaves, the low-calorie rice noodles form a nest for the shrimp and sugar snap peas. Crisp and naturally sweet, sugar snaps are cousin of the snow pea. Eat them, pod and all. If you grow your own sugar snaps, pick the pretty pea blossoms with tendrils for a garnish.

Oriental Dressing, see below
1 pound medium-size shrimp, cooked, cleaned
5 to 6 ounces sugar snap peas, strings removed, blanched 30 seconds,
   chilled in iced water, drained
6 ounces rice vermicelli, soaked in warm water 5 minutes
1 tablespoon safflower oil
2 tablespoons minced mint
2 tablespoons minced cilantro
2 tablespoons minced shiso leaves (perilla leaves)
1/4 cup finely chopped peanuts

Oriental Dressing:

1/3 cup rice vinegar
3/4 cup safflower oil
2 garlic cloves, finely minced
3 thin green onions, finely minced
1 teaspoon minced lemon grass or 1/2 teaspoon grated lemon peel
1-1/2 teaspoons sugar
1-1/2 teaspoons Southeast Asian fish sauce (page 111)
1/2 teaspoon salt, or to taste
1 rounded teaspoon hot chile sauce with garlic

Prepare Oriental Dressing. In a medium-size bowl, marinate shrimp with 1/2 cup dressing 30 minutes. Prepare sugar snaps. Stir into shrimp. Drain rice noodles. In a medium-size pot, bring 2 quarts water to a boil; add rice noodles. Cook 2 minutes or until tender yet firm to the bite. Drain and rinse with cool water. Drain again; press out excess water. Toss with oil, mint, cilantro and shiso in a large bowl. Spread noodles into a nest-shape on a serving platter. With a slotted spoon, remove shrimp and sugar snaps from marinade; place over rice sticks. Sprinkle with peanuts. Serve remaining dressing on the side. Makes 4 luncheon servings or 8 first-course servings.

Oriental Dressing

In a large bowl, whisk ingredients together. Makes about 1-1/3 cups.

Seafood Spaghetti in Tomato-Herb Sauce

*Be sure the clams are well-scrubbed and washed in cold water to remove
the sand in their shells. In the Naples area of Italy, one might be served spaghetti
topped with small clams still in their shells. After they are cooked, you can remove
them from their shells before they go into the sauce, if you prefer.*

12 little neck clams, scrubbed, rinsed in cold water
1/2 cup dry white vermouth
2 tablespoons extra-virgin olive oil
1 tablespoon butter
2 shallots, minced
3 garlic cloves, minced
3 ripe tomatoes, peeled, seeded, chopped (2 cups)
8 ounces large shrimp, peeled, deveined and cut into 3 pieces
5 to 6 ounces sea scallops, sliced in half
1 tablespoon fresh lemon juice
1 tablespoon each minced fresh parsley and basil
Salt and freshly ground pepper to taste
8 to 9 ounces spaghetti or linguini

Place clams in a medium-size skillet over medium-high heat, discarding any that do not close when tapped. Add wine. Cover pan; cook 5 to 6 minutes, shaking pan often. When clams open, remove pan from heat. Discard any which do not open. Keep warm. In a large skillet, heat olive oil and butter over medium heat. Sauté shallots and garlic 1 minute. Add tomatoes. Simmer 10 minutes. Add shrimp, scallops, lemon juice, herbs, salt and pepper. Simmer 1 to 2 minutes. Pour clams, still in their shells, into seafood mixture along with the pan broth. Shake pan to blend ingredients. Reduce heat to lowest setting; keep warm. In a large pot, bring 3 quarts water to a boil; add salt and spaghetti. Cook 8 to 10 minutes or until tender yet firm to the bite. Drain well. Place into a large warm bowl; add seafood sauce. Mix lightly. Serve on a large platter. Makes 3 or 4 servings.

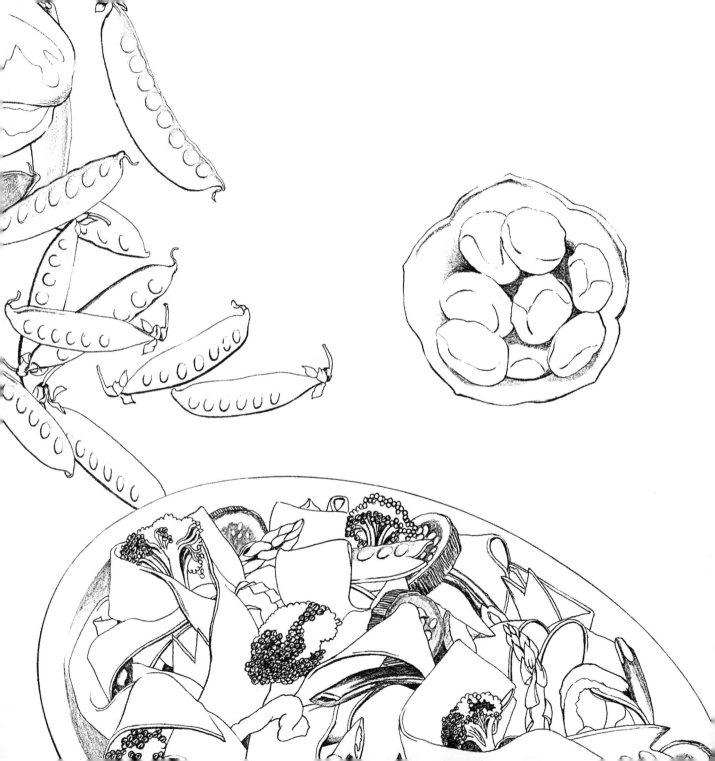

Noodles with Vegetables

You will never be at a loss for something good to eat if you have a box of spaghetti in the pantry and fresh vegetables in the refrigerator. With little fanfare, you can quickly create a satisfying dish that will please the family or unexpected guests. Sauté the sliced vegetables with a little garlic in olive oil. Toss in cooked spaghetti; sprinkle with cheese. The only thing left to do is to sit down and enjoy!

Also try this method with any long string noodles or flat-ribbon noodles you prefer. Sautéed onions, shallots, leeks, garlic or gingerroot provide a good seasoning base. Select one vegetable or several, which provide color, flavor and texture contrast. The vegetables can be blanched, sautéed, stir-fried, steamed, grilled, microwaved or cooked into a sauce before being mixed with the noodles. Add flavor accents such as wild mushrooms, olives, pine nuts, anchovies and sun-dried tomatoes. To appreciate the intensity of sun-dried tomatoes, try the Fusilli with Sun-dried Tomato & Eggplant Sauce (page 74). Fresh and dried herbs provide an additional flavor boost. Grated hard cheeses like Parmesan, pecorino Romano, asiago, kasseri and ricotta salata add a rich final touch. Cubes of softer cheeses can be stirred into the hot noodles; they become mellow and meltingly creamy.

Asian cooks are masters at combining vegetables and noodles. Follow their example and try stir-frying baby bok choy, black mushrooms and red bell pepper with garlic, gingerroot and a sprinkle of soy sauce. Toss in a handful of softened rice vermicelli or bean threads. Chinese egg noodles or eggless wheat noodles can be seasoned with an array of flavorful sauces based on ground bean pastes, ground nuts and seeds. The Chinese believe the world is in balance when the Five Elements (nature's energies) are in order. Your world will be in perfect order when you surprise your family with the colorful dish Five Precious Shreds (page 77). Rice noodles are tossed with five types of ginger-scented vegetable shreds. Offer this dish as an elegant side dish for Chinese barbecued chicken or turn it into a light main dish by adding tofu.

To increase the protein value of your noodle dishes, add nutritionally rich seeds, peanuts, almonds and beans. Combine them with delicious whole-grain pastas. Tagliatelle with White Beans, Zucchini & Bell Pepper (page 83) can be served as a light but satisfying main dish. Tofu is an economical source of protein, calcium and minerals. It tastes delicious when cubed and pan-fried until crispy. Serve small portions of bean-rich dishes such as chili or creamy cooked red beans over noodles. Dark leafy greens such as spinach, kale and Swiss chard are also excellent nutritional boosters.

Stir-fried Chinese Noodles with Vegetables

Use this basic recipe to stir-fry a quick dish of Chinese noodles. For a light meal, serve with egg-flower soup and a side-dish of pickled vegetables. You can also add additional vegetables such as bean sprouts, sliced mushrooms or bell pepper shreds. Vegetarians can add protein in the form of sautéed cubes of firm tofu. Non-vegetarians can add meat, chicken or seafood. This dish is similar to Japanese yaki soba.

8 to 9 ounces fresh Chinese noodles or 1 recipe Chinese Egg Noodles (page 8)
4 tablespoons vegetable oil
2 tablespoons light soy sauce
2 or 3 dashes white pepper
1 teaspoon finely minced fresh gingerroot
4 or 5 green onions, thinly sliced
2 garlic cloves, finely minced
3 cups shredded napa cabbage
1 small carrot, shredded

In a large pot, bring 3 quarts water to a boil; add noodles. Cook 2 minutes or until tender yet firm to the bite. Drain noodles. Rinse with cold water. Drain again. In a medium-size bowl, mix noodles with 1 tablespoon of the oil, the soy sauce and white pepper. Set aside. Heat a wok or heavy large skillet over medium heat. Add remaining oil. Add gingerroot, green onions and garlic and stir-fry 1 minute. Add cabbage and carrot. Stir-fry 1 to 2 minutes more. Reduce heat. Add noodles; toss with vegetable mixture. Taste for seasoning. Add additional soy sauce, pepper or salt, if desired. Makes 4 servings.

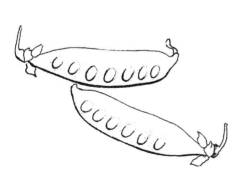

Spaghetti with Swiss Chard, Sun-dried Tomatoes & Fontina

Swiss chard is a nutritious green leafy vegetable loaded with vitamins and minerals. Related to spinach, the tender leaves cook quickly. It is delicious in this pasta dish, paired with tangy sun-dried tomatoes and cubes of creamy, melting fontina. Serve this dish for lunch or as a side dish for chicken or veal.

3 tablespoons butter
1 medium-size onion, chopped
2 large garlic cloves, minced
3 large Swiss chard leaves, rinsed, stalks removed, rolled and thinly sliced (about 3 cups)
3/4 cup chicken stock
1/2 cup whipping cream
1/2 cup sun-dried tomato halves, rehydrated, cut into strips (about 1 oz.)
Dash ground nutmeg
Salt and freshly ground pepper to taste
8 ounces spaghetti
4 ounces Italian fontina cheese, Bel Paese cheese or mozzarella cheese, cut into 1/4-inch cubes

In a medium-size saucepan, melt butter over medium heat. Add onion and garlic and sauté 4 minutes or until soft. Add chard; cook, stirring, 1 minute. Add stock. Cook 2 minutes. Add cream, tomatoes and nutmeg. Simmer mixture 4 to 5 minutes. Add salt and pepper. Keep warm. In a large pot, bring 3 quarts water to a boil; add salt and spaghetti. Cook 8 to 10 minutes or until tender yet firm to the bite. Drain spaghetti; mix into the sauce. Stir in cheese; heat 1 minute or just until cheese cubes soften. Serve at once. Makes 4 first-course servings.

Fusilli with Sun-dried Tomato & Eggplant Sauce

Imported sun-dried tomato paste or concentrate is conveniently sold in tubes. Not meant as a substitute for fresh tomatoes, it is used in small amounts to add a rich tomato flavor to your dishes. Purchase it in Italian markets and gourmet shops. Refrigerate paste after opening.

3 tablespoons vegetable oil
2 (4-oz.) purple Oriental eggplants, sliced diagonally 1/4 inch thick
1 tablespoon butter
3 shallots, minced
2 garlic cloves, minced
4 plum tomatoes, peeled, seeded and diced
2 tablespoons tomato concentrate or tomato paste
1/2 cup chicken stock
1/2 cup sun-dried tomatoes, rehydrated, coarsely chopped (about 1 oz.)
1 tablespoon minced fresh Italian parsley
1 tablespoon minced fresh oregano or basil or 1 teaspoon dried leaf basil or oregano
1/4 cup whipping cream
1 teaspoon sugar
1/4 teaspoon salt, or to taste
Freshly ground pepper to taste
6 ounces fusilli (corkscrew-shaped pasta), or gemelli
1/3 cup freshly grated pecorino Romano or Parmesan cheese

In a large skillet, heat 1 tablespoon of the oil over medium heat. Spread eggplant slices in a single layer. Cook until lightly browned. Turn slices; drizzle with 1 tablespoon oil. When browned, remove from pan and set aside. Add remaining oil and butter to skillet. Sauté shallots and garlic 2 to 3 minutes or until soft. Add plum tomatoes, tomato concentrate and stock. Reduce heat; simmer 3 minutes. Stir in sun-dried tomatoes, herbs, cream, sugar and reserved eggplant. Add salt and pepper. Simmer 3 or 4 minutes. Keep warm. In a large pot, bring 3 quarts water to a boil; add salt and fusilli. Cook 8 to 10 minutes or until tender yet firm to the bite. Drain noodles; place into a large bowl. Mix in tomato sauce. Divide between serving plates. Sprinkle with Romano cheese. Makes 3 or 4 side-dish servings.

Three-Pepper Pasta

Gemelli, or "twins," resembles two skinny short pieces of spaghetti twisted together. This colorful sauce would also be good over spaghetti-length corkscrew fusilli or linguini. Sweet red bell peppers have a special flavor when roasted. Roast under the broiler or over a charcoal grill until blistered and charred. Sweat in a paper bag about twenty minutes, then peel, seed and use as desired.

3 large red bell peppers, roasted, peeled and seeded
2 tablespoons extra-virgin olive oil
2 tablespoons butter
1 medium-size onion, finely chopped
3 garlic cloves, minced
3/4 cup chicken stock
2 tablespoons minced fresh Italian parsley
1 tablespoon minced fresh tarragon or 1 teaspoon dried leaf tarragon
Dried hot red pepper flakes to taste
Salt and ground white pepper to taste
8 ounces dried gemelli or fusilli
About 1/2 cup freshly grated Parmesan cheese

Dice bell peppers. Heat oil and butter in a large skillet over medium heat. Add onion and sauté 4 minutes. Add garlic; cook 30 seconds. Add bell peppers and stock. Simmer 5 minutes. Stir in herbs, hot pepper flakes, salt and white pepper; keep warm. In a large pot, bring 3 quarts water to a boil; add salt and gemelli. Cook 8 to 10 minutes or until tender yet firm to the bite. Drain well. Arrange noodles in a large heated bowl. Stir in pepper mixture and cheese. Makes 4 side-dish or 2 main-dish servings.

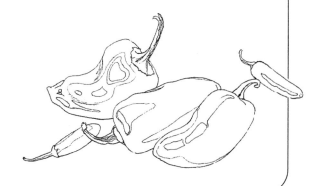

Linguini & Broccoli in Spicy Garlic Oil

Linguini is flat spaghetti. This easy dish is appreciated in Naples, Italy, where simplicity, economy and good taste are highly valued. Substitute any fresh vegetable you have on hand. I like to make this dish the day after a party, when there are leftover cut-up vegetables from the dip tray. Try cauliflower, zucchini, carrots or a combination of all three. Serve as a great side-dish with grilled chicken or steak.

8 ounces linguini or spaghetti
3 cups small broccoli flowerets, blanched 1 minute, chilled in iced water
1/4 cup extra-virgin olive oil
4 large garlic cloves, smashed
1 small fresh chile, sliced in half, seeds removed
2 tablespoons minced fresh Italian parsley
About 1/2 cup freshly grated Parmesan cheese or Romano cheese

In a large pot, bring 3 quarts water to a boil; add linguini. Cook 8 to 10 minutes or until tender yet firm to the bite. Drain well. Pat broccoli dry on paper towels. In a large skillet, heat oil over medium-low heat. Add garlic and chile. Cook slowly, stirring, until garlic turns golden-brown. Do not allow garlic to burn. Discard garlic and chile. Stir in broccoli; cook 1 to 2 minutes. Add linguini and parsley. Toss ingredients. Sprinkle each portion with grated cheese. Makes 4 or 5 side-dish servings.

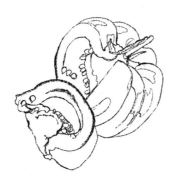

Five Precious Shreds

Fresh julienned vegetables are stir-fried in ginger-scented oil, then tossed with bean threads. Texture is highly valued in China. The Chinese appreciate the crunchy taste of the vegetables and the chewy resilience of bean threads. Sautéed strips of tofu can be added to create a protein-rich dish. Angel hair pasta or cappellini can be substituted for bean threads.

4 ounces bean threads or Korean soba, soaked in warm water 20 minutes
1 medium-size carrot, cut into julienne strips
1 small red bell pepper, cut into julienne strips
2 ounces snow peas, ends trimmed, cut into julienne strips
6 green onions, smashed, shredded
8 ounces fresh bean sprouts
3 tablespoons vegetable oil
4 (1/8-inch-thick) slices gingerroot, smashed
2 garlic cloves, minced
2 tablespoons minced fresh cilantro
1 teaspoon sesame oil
1 teaspoon sugar
1/2 teaspoon salt
2 tablespoons toasted sesame seeds
Soy sauce, if desired

Drain bean threads. Place in a medium-size bowl. Cover with boiling water; soak 5 minutes. Drain and rinse with cool water. Press out excess water. Heat a wok or large skillet over medium heat. Add oil. Add gingerroot and stir-fry 1 to 2 minutes or until it turns light brown. Discard from oil. Add carrot, bell pepper and garlic. Stir-fry 1 minute. Add snow peas, green onions and bean sprouts. Stir-fry 1 to 2 minutes. Reduce heat. Mix in cilantro, sesame oil, sugar and salt. Add bean threads; blend with ingredients. Season with soy sauce to taste, if desired. Remove to serving platter. Sprinkle with sesame seeds. Makes 4 side-dish servings.

Egg Noodles & Cheese with Fresh Herbs & Pecans

This creamy noodle dish is pure comfort food. It contains just enough gorgonzola cheese to lend an intriguing flavor. The crunchy bite of pecans add a nice textural contrast. Serve the noodles as a meal-in-a-dish with a green salad on the side.

3 ounces cream cheese, room temperature
2 tablespoons butter, room temperature
1/2 cup dairy sour cream, room temperature
1 cup ricotta cheese or creamy cottage cheese
2 tablespoons freshly grated Parmesan cheese
1 tablespoon each minced fresh parsley, snipped chives, parsley or marjoram
4 ounces medium-size dried egg noodles
1/3 cup whipping cream
2 ounces gorgonzola cheese or blue cheese, crumbled
1/4 teaspoon salt
Freshly ground pepper to taste
1/3 cup chopped toasted pecans or walnuts

In a medium-size bowl, blend cream cheese, butter and sour cream until smooth. Stir in ricotta cheese, Parmesan cheese and herbs. In a large pot, bring 3 quarts water to a boil; add noodles. Cook 6 to 7 minutes or until tender yet firm to the bite. Drain well. Place back into the pot; stir in cheese mixture and whipping cream. Mix in gorgonzola cheese. Add salt and pepper. Sprinkle each serving with pecans. Makes 3 main-dish servings or 5 or 6 side-dish servings.

Carrot Ribbon Noodles with Wild Mushroom Sauce

Delicate spice-scented carrot pasta and fragrant mushroom sauce with marjoram and chives are a winning combination. Serve this magical dish to someone special in your life. Folklore says sweet marjoram was created by Venus to heal a wound caused by Cupid's dart. Romanian gypsies are rumored to have used chives in creating incantations and spells.

1 recipe Carrot Ribbon Noodles (page 11) or 8 ounces fresh fettuccine
1 tablespoon butter
1 tablespoon vegetable oil
12 ounces fresh mushrooms (shiitake, oyster, chanterelle or button), sliced
2 shallots, finely minced
1 garlic clove, finely minced
1/2 cup chicken stock
3/4 cup whipping cream
Salt and freshly ground pepper to taste
1 tablespoon each chopped fresh marjoram and snipped fresh chives
3 tablespoons toasted pine nuts

Prepare Carrot Ribbon Noodles. In a medium-size saucepan, heat butter and oil over medium-high heat. Add mushrooms, shallots and garlic; sauté 2 to 3 minutes. Pour in chicken stock and cream. Reduce heat; simmer 4 to 5 minutes or until slightly reduced. Stir in salt, pepper and herbs. Keep warm. Bring 3 quarts water to a boil in a large pot; add salt and noodles. Cook 1 to 2 minutes or until tender yet firm to the bite. Drain well; place in a medium-size bowl. Add warm sauce; toss to combine. Divide among plates; sprinkle with pine nuts. Makes 2 main-dish servings or 4 first-course servings.

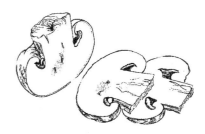

Spaghetti with Cherry Tomatoes, Olives & Fresh Herbs

Simple and delicious! When you are short on time and want to whip up something delicious, try this quick spaghetti dish. You can use red or yellow cherry tomatoes. A combination of the two would be spectacular. Serve the spaghetti as a side dish or light meal.

1/4 cup butter
3 garlic cloves, minced
25 cherry tomatoes, cut in half
1/3 cup brine-cured ripe olives, cut into quarters and pitted
Hot pepper flakes to taste
1 tablespoon each minced fresh parsley, snipped fresh chives and fresh basil
Salt and freshly ground pepper to taste
8 ounces thin spaghetti
About 1/2 cup grated pecorino Romano cheese or ricotta salata cheese

In a large skillet, melt butter over medium heat. Add garlic and sauté 30 seconds. Add tomatoes; sauté 1 minute or until hot. Stir in olives, pepper flakes and herbs. Keep warm. In a large pot, bring 3 quarts water to a boil; add spaghetti. Cook 4 to 6 minutes or until tender yet firm to the bite. Drain well. Combine with the tomato mixture. Add salt and pepper. Serve with grated cheese. Makes 4 or 5 servings.

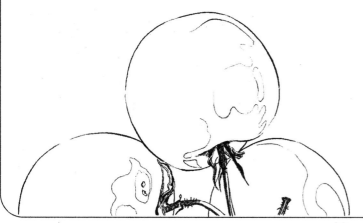

Korean Noodles & Vegetables with Red Pepper Sauce

Korean noodles are a symbol of longevity, enjoyed during special occasions to facilitate long life and happiness. This refreshing dish features thin wheat noodles called son myon, but soba could be used as well. Naeng-myon, or Korean soba, is a chewy, long brown buckwheat noodle. In Seoul, it was fascinating to see restaurant waitresses using scissors to snip unmanageably long noodles right on the customers' plates.

1 recipe Korean Red Pepper Sauce (page 14)
12 ounces Korean, Japanese, or Chinese thin wheat noodles or Korean soba
1 tablespoon sesame oil
1 carrot, cut into julienne strips, blanched 30 seconds, chilled
1 cup bean sprouts, blanched 30 seconds, rinsed in cold water, drained
2 eggs, beaten, fried into a thin round egg sheet, shredded
8 ounces fresh spinach, blanched 30 seconds, drained, gently squeezed dry
3 green onions, shredded diagonally
1 tablespoon toasted sesame seeds

Prepare Korean Red Pepper Sauce. In a large pot, bring 4 quarts water to a boil; add noodles. Cook 3 to 4 minutes or until tender yet firm to the bite. Drain; rinse under cool water. Drain again. Coat with sesame oil. Divide noodles among large noodle bowls. On top of each portion, arrange 1/4 of the carrot, bean sprouts, shredded egg, spinach and green onions. Sprinkle with sesame seeds. Before eating, let each diner mix pepper sauce to taste into individual portions of noodles and vegetables. Makes 4 servings.

Variation

For a nonvegetarian dish, top each bowl of noodles with 2 slices Braised Szechuan Pork Roast (page 32) or Chinese Roast Pork (page 42).

Bucatini with Garlic, Sun-dried Tomatoes & Ripe Olives

Bucatini is the Roman name for fat, hollow spaghetti with a hole through the center. My first taste of bucatini came inside pasta care packages sent from my sister in Italy. This quick, easy dish contains fried bread crumbs, used as a cheese substitute for reasons of economy. This is a good way to use up leftover dry pieces of bread. Chopped anchovies or chopped, sautéed pancetta would be tasty additions to this dish.

1 tablespoon butter
8 tablespoons extra-virgin olive oil
3/4 cup Italian or French bread crumbs
1 medium-size red onion, chopped
4 garlic cloves, minced
2 tablespoons minced fresh Italian parsley or regular parsley
2 tablespoons minced fresh basil
1/2 cup sun-dried tomatoes, rehydrated, chopped (about 1 oz.)
20 oil-packed ripe olives, pitted, chopped
8 ounces bucatini or spaghetti
Salt and freshly ground pepper to taste
1/2 cup freshly grated pecorino Romano cheese or Parmesan cheese

In a small skillet, heat butter and 1 tablespoon of the oil over medium heat. Add bread crumbs; sauté until crisp and golden. Set aside. In a large skillet, heat remaining oil over medium heat. Add onion; cook 4 minutes. Add garlic; cook 2 minutes more. Stir in fresh herbs, tomatoes and olives. Cook mixture 1 to 2 minutes. Reduce heat; keep warm. Bring 3 quarts water to a boil in a large pot; add bucatini. Cook 10 to 12 minutes or until tender yet firm to the bite. Drain well. Stir into skillet mixture. Add salt and pepper. Stir in 1/4 cup toasted bread crumbs. Top each serving with cheese and additional bread crumbs. Makes 4 servings.

Tagliatelle with White Beans, Zucchini & Bell Pepper

The great soups of Italy often contain pasta and beans. Here, they are combined with fresh sautéed zucchini, bell pepper and fresh herbs to create a nutritious, economical dish. A nice accompaniment would be sliced fresh tomatoes. Cannelini beans add character to this simple dish. If you use canned beans, rinse and drain well before adding them to the skillet.

3 tablespoons olive oil
1 small red onion, chopped
2 garlic cloves, minced
3 cups small, fresh zucchini slices, cut into strips
1/2 red bell pepper, diced
1-1/4 cups cooked cannellini beans (white kidney beans) or great northern beans
1 tablespoon minced fresh savory, oregano or basil
1 tablespoon minced fresh Italian parsley
1 recipe Basic Egg Noodles (page 6) cut into tagliatelle or 8 to 9 ounces fresh fettuccine
Salt and freshly ground pepper to taste
About 1/2 cup freshly grated pecorino Romano cheese or Parmesan cheese

Heat oil in a large skillet over medium heat. Add onion and garlic and sauté 2 minutes. Add zucchini and bell pepper; cook 4 to 5 minutes or until vegetables soften. Stir in beans and herbs; cook 1 minute. Keep warm. Bring 3 quarts water to a boil in a large pot; add salt and tagliatelle. Cook 1 to 2 minutes or until tender yet firm to the bite. Drain well. Toss with vegetable mixture. Add salt and pepper. Divide among serving plates. Top with grated cheese. Makes 2 or 3 main-dish servings or 4 side-dish servings.

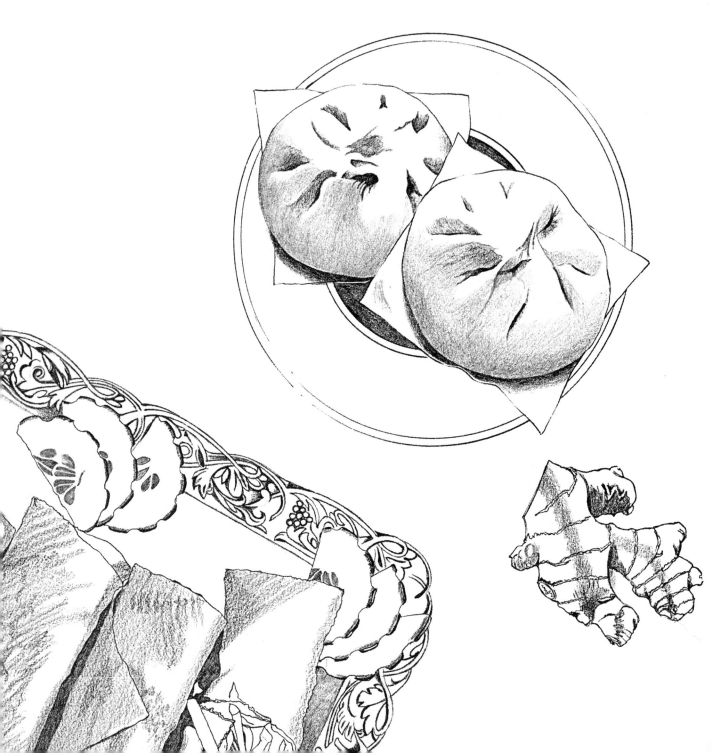

Stuffed, Wrapped & Rolled Noodles

Noodle dough can be rolled into many shapes besides long ribbons and strings. Sheets of dough can be cut into square or circular wrappers in various sizes for stuffing and rolling. Good-quality commercial wrappers can be conveniently purchased in grocery stores and Asian markets. In this chapter you will find delicious recipes for turning these wrappers into pastries and dumplings, which are stuffed, wrapped and rolled. Serve these small delights as appetizers, snacks or part of a multi-course meal. Most of them can be made ahead of time and refrigerated before cooking; others can be frozen for later use.

Dumplings share a homespun universality like few other foods. Their ancient origins are from China. Dumplings were basically peasant food, made by ingenious Asian cooks who had to get by with ingredients on hand. Small bits of meat and vegetables can be stretched a long way when stuffed in noodle wrappers and boiled in water. Many times in Asia, I have eaten dumplings like the Spicy Chinese Dumplings with Red Chile Sauce on page 88. Bursting with flavor, these boiled dumplings are extremely versatile. They can be pan-fried or deep-fried, depending on the whim of the cook. Add them to chicken soup, or season them with spicy Red Chile Sauce (page 15).

In one form or another, dumplings are popular around the world. Turkish Borek, Tartar Style (page 86) are stuffed with lamb, served with cool yogurt-garlic sauce, then drizzled with sizzling-hot chile butter. In Saudi Arabia, one might sample Bahdria's Arabian Lamb Crescents (page 92).

Asian cooks roll meat, seafood and vegetable fillings inside dough wrappers, then deep-fry them into crisp snacks that are a favorite food at New Year's time when the Chinese lunar calendar falls at the opening of Spring. Some of these small "meals-in-a-wrapper" are not fried but eaten out-of-hand like a fresh taco. Vietnamese Crab & Shrimp Spring Rolls (page 90) have a unique crispy wrapper made from softened rice paper dough.

The Chinese serve small pastries like these at *yum cha,* or high tea. They are called *dim sum,* or foods which "touch the heart." Tea houses are noisy, hospitable restaurants where families and business acquaintances gather at round tables in a culinary celebration of everyday life. Do as the Asians do and invite family and friends to come and socialize while sharing the fun of stuffing, wrapping and rolling these small exquisite treats. The highlight of the party always comes, of course, when the pastries have been cooked and the feasting begins!

Turkish Borek, Tartar Style

Borek consists of a group of meat and cheese-filled flaky pastries created by the ancient Turks of Central Asia. Tartar-style borek are poached dumplings stuffed with a meat-and-dill mixture. The dumplings are enriched with a garlicky yogurt sauce and melted butter.

Yogurt Sauce, see below
Meat Filling, see below
1 (16-oz.) package won-ton wrappers
1/2 cup unsalted butter, melted
1 teaspoon hot red pepper flakes
2 tablespoons chicken-flavored bouillon granules

Yogurt Sauce:

1-1/2 cups plain yogurt
1/2 teaspoon salt
2 garlic cloves, minced
2 green onions, minced

Meat Filling:

1 pound lean ground lamb or beef
1 small onion, minced
2 garlic cloves, minced
2 tablespoons minced fresh dill or 1 tablespoon dried dill weed
1/3 cup minced fresh parsley
3/4 teaspoon salt
1/8 teaspoon freshly ground pepper

Prepare Yogurt Sauce. Prepare Meat Filling. Place 1 teaspoon filling in center of each wrapper. Moisten edges with water. Pull up 2 corners of the wrapper to form a triangle; press tightly. Pull up other 2 corners. Press the 4 corners tightly together, then press the 4 sides tightly to seal. Keep dumpling bundles covered. In a small saucepan, melt butter with pepper flakes; keep warm. In a large pot, bring 3 quarts water and bouillon granules to a boil. Add 1/2 of the dumplings to the broth; reduce heat and simmer 2 to 3 minutes. Dumplings will float when done. With a slotted spoon,

remove dumplings to a buttered serving bowl; keep warm. Cook remaining dumplings. Serve in shallow bowls, topped with spoonfuls of Yogurt Sauce. Drizzle with pepper-butter. Makes 5 or 6 servings.

Yogurt Sauce

In a medium-size bowl, combine all ingredients. Makes about 1-1/2 cups.

Meat Filling

In a medium-size bowl, mix all ingredients well.

Spicy Chinese Dumplings with Red Chile Sauce

Dumplings have been a staple food in Northern China for over one thousand years.
Preserved dumplings have been excavated from eighth century tombs on the "old silk road."
Do not overcook dumplings; wrappers become too soft. If gyoza skins are unavailable,
substitute won-ton wrappers trimmed into circles or left in square shapes.

Red Chile Sauce (page 15)
Meat Filling, see below
1 tablespoon cornstarch
1 tablespoon water
1 (10-oz.) package round Japanese gyoza skins
2 tablespoons chicken-flavored bouillon granules
1/4 cup torn cilantro leaves

Meat Filling:

1 pound lean ground pork or beef
1 cup minced cabbage, blanched in boiling water 1 minute, drained
2 tablespoons dry white wine
1/4 cup water
1 tablespoon soy sauce
1 large garlic clove, finely minced
1 tablespoon minced gingerroot
2 green onions, finely minced
1/2 teaspoon sesame oil
1/4 teaspoon ground pepper

Prepare Red Chile Sauce. Prepare Meat Filling. In a small bowl, blend cornstarch and 1 tablespoon water. Place 1 heaping teaspoon meat mixture in the center of each skin. Moisten edges with cornstarch mixture. Fold skins in half, forming semicircles. Press edges tightly together. Place dumplings on a tray, pressing bottoms to slightly flatten. Keep dumplings covered. In a large pot, bring 3 quarts water and the bouillon granules to a boil. Add 1/3 of the dumplings to the broth; reduce heat and simmer 1 to 2 minutes. Dumplings will float when done. With a slotted spoon, remove to a large serving platter coated lightly with oil. Keep warm; cook remaining dumplings. Pour sauce over dumplings in platter; garnish with cilantro. Makes 4 or 5 main-dish servings or 8 to 10 appetizer servings.

Meat Filling

In a medium-size bowl, mix all ingredients well.

Variation

Pan-fried Dumplings: To fry dumplings instead of boiling, add 1 tablespoon vegetable oil to a large nonstick skillet heated over medium-high heat. Add dumplings, bottom or flat-side down. Fry the bottoms of the dumplings 1 to 2 minutes until golden-brown. Pour 1/4 cup beef or chicken stock into skillet. Add lid; steam 2 minutes or until the skins are translucent and meat is no longer pink.

Vietnamese Crab & Shrimp Spring Rolls

Cha gio are made with softened rice paper wrappers which have a special crispness when fried. Do not fry spring rolls at too high a temperature; the wrappers will cook before the filling. Fried spring rolls can be wrapped in tender lettuce leaves with sprigs of fresh cilantro, mint and basil tucked inside. Dip into dressing before eating. If triangular wrappers are unavailable, cut twelve-inch wrappers into quarters or use six-inch wrappers.

Filling, see below
28 triangular rice papers
1 egg, slightly beaten
4 cups vegetable oil for deep-frying
Vietnamese Chile-Lime Dressing (page 16)

Filling:

1 ounce bean threads, soaked in water 10 minutes, cut into 1-inch pieces
2 tablespoons dried tree ears, soaked in water 30 minutes, rinsed, drained and chopped
1 cup bean sprouts
8 ounces ground pork
6 ounces medium-size shrimp, peeled, deveined and chopped
4 ounces cooked crabmeat
1 egg
2 shallots, minced
2 garlic cloves, minced
1 teaspoon sugar
2 teaspoons Southeast Asian fish sauce (page 111)
1/4 teaspoon salt
1/4 teaspoon freshly ground pepper

Prepare Filling. Dip 1/3 of the rice papers quickly in and out of a shallow pan of water. Shake dry; lay on a flat surface, pointed ends up. Allow to soften 3 or 4 minutes. Brush top sides lightly with egg. Place 2 tablespoons filling in the center of each triangle. Fold sides over; roll up from the bottom to form a cylinder. Moisten outside flap with egg to insure a good seal. Dip and fill remaining wrappers. Spring rolls can be tightly covered and refrigerated several hours before frying. In a wok or a heavy, medium-size skillet, heat oil to 350°F (175°C). Fry a few rolls at a time, turning often, until crisp and golden. Drain well. Serve with dressing as a dipping sauce. Makes 6 appetizer servings.

Filling

In a large bowl, mix ingredients together until well blended.

Chocolate Date-Filled Crescents

Chocolate noodle dough crescents are stuffed with an orange-date filling, then deep-fried until crisp. Dust the fried chocolate crescents with powdered sugar or granulated sugar, if desired. Serve plain or with your favorite fruity dipping sauce.

Orange-Date Paste, see below
1 recipe Chocolate Noodle Sheets (page 9) rolled into 1/16 inch thick
Cornstarch for dusting
4 cups peanut oil for deep-frying
1 egg, slightly beaten
Sugar (optional)

Orange-Date Paste:

8 ounces pitted dates, cut into small pieces
1/2 cup orange juice
1 tablespoon grated orange peel
1/4 cup sugar
1/4 cup shredded coconut
2 tablespoons chopped walnuts

Prepare Orange-Date Paste. Prepare Chocolate Noodle Sheets. With a sharp-edge round cutter, cut dough into about 32 (3-inch) circles. Dust with cornstarch; stack and keep covered. In a wok or heavy, medium-size skillet, heat oil to 375°F (190°C). Place 1/2 teaspoon date paste in the center of each wrapper. Moisten inside edges with beaten egg; press to seal. Fry crescents 2 minutes or until crisp. Drain on a wire rack. Coat with sugar, if desired. Serve at once. Makes about 32 crescents.

Orange-Date Paste

In a medium-size saucepan, simmer dates, orange juice, orange peel and sugar 10 minutes or until mixture forms a dry paste. Stir in coconut and walnuts. Cool completely. Makes about 1 cup.

Bahdria's Arabian Lamb Crescents

Sambosas are deep-fried lamb-and-parsley-stuffed pastry crescents. I learned to make them from a special friend from Riyadh, Saudi Arabia. Bahdria uses whole-wheat Middle Eastern dough for the wrappers; substitute won-ton wrappers trimmed in circles, or Japanese gyoza wrappers. I like to serve the pastries with Pineapple Sweet-Sour Sauce (page 17).

8 ounces ground lamb
1 egg yolk
3 green onions, finely minced
1 garlic clove, finely minced
1 teaspoon ground cumin
1/3 cup minced fresh parsley
1/4 teaspoon salt
Freshly ground pepper to taste
8 ounces won-ton wrappers (about 30)
1 egg, slightly beaten
3 cups peanut or vegetable oil for deep-frying

In a medium-size bowl, combine lamb with all the remaining ingredients except won-ton wrappers, whole egg and peanut oil. Cut won-ton wrappers into circles with a 3-inch-round cutter or with scissors. Place a wrapper on a flat surface. Place 1 heaping teaspoon filling in the center. Moisten edge of pastry with egg; press firmly to seal. Fill remaining crescents; keep covered. In a wok or heavy, medium-size skillet, heat oil to 360°F (175°C). Fry crescents 2 minutes, turning often, until crisp and golden. Drain on a wire rack. Serve with sauce. Makes 5 or 6 appetizer servings.

Shrimp, Sweet Potato & Green Bean Lumpia

Sweet potatoes and green beans taste sensational in Filipino-style spring rolls. Fried paper-thin, lumpia skins are crisper than the regular egg-roll wrappers found in American markets. They seem delicate, but the skins can be purchased frozen, thawed and re-frozen at home with no ill effects.

Garlic & Vinegar Dipping Sauce (page 15)
8 ounces medium-size shrimp, peeled, deveined and finely chopped
1 tablespoon dry white wine
2 teaspoons cornstarch
4 cups plus 1 tablespoon vegetable oil
1 medium-size red onion, chopped
3 garlic cloves, minced
8 ounces ground pork
1 cup sweet potato cubes, cut into 1/4-inch squares, parboiled until tender
4 ounces tender young green beans, cut into 1-1/2-inch strips, blanched
1 cup shredded napa cabbage
1 cup fresh bean sprouts
2 tablespoons soy sauce
1 tablespoon sugar
Salt and freshly ground pepper to taste
1/3 cup chicken stock
20 lumpia wrappers or spring-roll wrappers

Prepare dipping sauce; set aside. In a small bowl, marinate shrimp in wine and 1 teaspoon of the cornstarch 10 minutes. In a wok or large skillet, heat the 1 tablespoon oil over medium-high heat. Add onion, garlic and pork and stir-fry 4 or 5 minutes. Drain shrimp; add to skillet. Cook 1 minute. Add sweet potato and green beans, cabbage and bean sprouts; cook 1 minute. Season with soy sauce, sugar, salt and pepper. In a small bowl, combine remaining cornstarch and stock. Pour into a well in the middle of the pan. Stir-fry until mixture becomes glazed. Cool mixture before using as a filling. To shape lumpia, place a wrapper on a flat surface. Spoon 3 tablespoons filling in an oblong shape along the bottom third of the wrapper. Fold bottom edge over filling; tuck under. Fold in sides; roll into a cylinder. Seal edge with water. Fill remaining lumpia; keep covered. In a wok or heavy, medium-size skillet, heat the 4 cups oil to 365°F (185°C). Fry a few lumpia at a time, until crisp and golden-brown. Drain well. Serve with sauce. Makes 8 to 10 appetizer servings.

Cantonese Tea-Lunch Chicken Noodle Rolls

Rice noodle rolls are always included in the dim sum selection at Chinese tea houses. They are stuffed with a variety of savory fillings. Any stir-fry with finely-chopped ingredients can be rolled inside a rice noodle sheet. Diced Chinese sausage or minced Oriental black mushrooms would be flavorful additions. Dip these tasty morsels into a mixture of soy sauce and sesame oil or the spicy Red Chile Sauce (page 15).

Oyster Sauce Glaze, see below
2 tablespoons vegetable oil
4 green onions, finely minced
1 teaspoon minced fresh gingerroot
1 large garlic clove, minced
1/4 cup finely minced water chestnuts
1 whole chicken breast, skinned, boned, finely minced
1 pound market rice noodle sheets or 1 recipe Homemade Rice Noodles (page 3)
1 tablespoon toasted sesame seeds

Oyster Sauce Glaze:

1 tablespoon soy sauce
1 tablespoon oyster sauce
1 teaspoon hot chile sauce
1 teaspoon sesame oil
1 teaspoon white vinegar
1 teaspoon sugar
2 teaspoons cornstarch

Prepare Oyster Sauce Glaze. Heat a wok or large skillet over medium heat. Add oil. Reserve 1 tablespoon green onion. Stir-fry remaining green onions, gingerroot, garlic and water chestnuts 1 minute. Add chicken; stir-fry until crumbly and no longer pink. Reduce heat slightly; add glaze. Stir-fry 1 minute until mixture has thickened slightly. Cool completely. Place 1 noodle sheet on a lightly oiled surface. Spoon about 1/4 cup chicken filling along the bottom edge of the noodle sheet. Roll up the sheet, enclosing filling. Fill remaining noodle sheets. Steam stuffed rolls over boiling water 10 minutes or until hot and pliable. Rolls made from homemade noodles do not need to be steamed after shaping. Rolls can be shaped, wrapped tightly and refrigerated 1 day before steaming. After steaming, sprinkle with reserved green onion and sesame seeds. Slice into 3/4-inch pieces. Serve with desired dipping sauce. Makes 3 or 4 servings.

Oyster Sauce Glaze

In a small bowl, combine all ingredients.

Crespelle Stuffed with Mushrooms, Spinach & Prosciutto

Crespelle, or thin Italian crepes, are categorized within the family of Italian noodles and pasta. The crespelle are spread with mushroom-spinach filling, folded and topped with béchamel and Romano cheese for glazing. The crespelle can also be rolled with a variety of other fillings and sauced with Bolognese sauce or fresh tomato sauce.

1 recipe Crespelle (page 10)
6 tablespoons butter
3 shallots, minced
3 large garlic cloves, minced
4 cups chopped fresh mushrooms (1 pound)
8 ounces fresh spinach, rinsed, blanched 30 seconds, squeezed dry and chopped
3/4 cup dairy sour cream or ricotta cheese
2 ounces prosciutto or Smithfield ham, chopped
Salt and freshly ground pepper to taste
2 tablespoons all-purpose flour
2 cups milk, heated until hot
1/2 teaspoon salt
Freshly grated nutmeg
1 cup freshly grated pecorino Romano or Parmesan cheese

Prepare Crespelle. In a large skillet, melt 3 tablespoons of the butter over medium-high heat; add shallots and garlic and sauté 30 seconds. Add mushrooms; cook until soft. If necessary, continue cooking to reduce excess liquid. Mix in spinach, sour cream and prosciutto. Add salt and pepper. Cool mixture. In a 2-1/2-quart saucepan over medium heat, melt remaining butter. Stir in flour; cook 2 minutes without browning. Whisk in milk; cook 2 to 3 minutes or until mixture simmers and thickens. Add 1/2 teaspoon salt, pepper and nutmeg. Preheat oven to 375°F (190°C). Place a crespella on a flat surface. Spread with 2 tablespoons filling; fold in half. Fold in half again to form a wedge-shape or 1/4 of a circle. Fill remaining crespelle. Arrange crespelle, overlapping, in a large circular casserole dish. Top with sauce; sprinkle with pecorino cheese. Bake 10 minutes, then cook under the broiler 2 to 3 minutes or until crispy and golden-brown. Makes 4 luncheon servings or 6 first-course servings.

Noodle Salads

Everyone loves a good salad—especially those made with noodles! Noodle salads are really a development of American ingenuity and are rarely seen in traditional Oriental or European cuisine. This chapter will provide you with a kaleidoscope of colorful, delicious noodle salads made with a wide range of international noodles such as fusilli corkscrews, buckwheat noodles, crispy won-ton noodles and instant ramen. The salads are simple to prepare, yet sophisticated enough to grace your most elegant table or buffet.

When making noodle salads, it is important to invest in the best ingredients you can buy. Imported semolina noodles and pasta hold their shape and texture better in salads than some domestic brands and better than most soft home-made noodles. Top-quality extra-virgin olive oil and light salad oils are especially important in salad-making where there is little or no cooking to mask their true flavors. The colors and textures of vegetables are important. Select fresh, young vegetables and blanch them just enough to remove the raw taste and enhance their bright colors.

Feel free to experiment with different types of noodles, but select those with shapes similar to those recommended in the recipes. Rice vermicelli, bean threads and Korean soba are interchangeable. Thin whole-wheat noodles can be substituted for Japanese buckwheat soba. Crispy Won-Ton Vermicelli (page 12) can be tossed in salads in place of crispy fried rice vermicelli or bean threads.

When cooking noodles for salad, boil them only until al dente or "firm to the bite." The noodles will continue absorbing the dressing, softening further. If you plan to combine the dressing and noodles ahead of time, you should reserve a portion of the dressing to add just before serving. The noodles will have absorbed most of the dressing while sitting, lessening its special flavor. Noodle salads taste better at room temperature but if you serve them chilled, you may need to adjust the seasonings. Chilling lessens their flavor intensity.

Several salads such as the Smoked Chicken, Broccoli & Pine Nuts with Fried Rice Noodles (page 101) or the Sesame-Almond Noodles (page 103) can star at your table as a spectacular luncheon dish or casual supper dish. Complete the meal with crusty bread and a platter of assorted cheeses and fruits. Served in small portions, any of the noodle salads would make a spectacular side dish or an impressive first-course offering.

Crunchy Noodle Coleslaw with Ginger Dressing

This is Oriental fun food! The unusual coleslaw is a medley of tiny noodle ringlets, marinated cabbage shreds and chopped almonds. It features instant ramen noodles which soften in the salad without precooking. Fresh minced dill weed or parsley could be substituted for cilantro. Double recipe or cut in half as needed.

Ginger Dressing, see below
4 cups thinly shredded cabbage
2 tablespoons shredded carrot
2 tablespoons toasted sesame seeds
2 green onions, minced
1/4 cup packed minced cilantro
2 (3-1/2-oz.) packages instant ramen noodles (discard seasoning packet)
1/4 cup chopped roasted almonds

Ginger Dressing:

1/2 cup safflower oil
3 tablespoons rice vinegar
1 rounded tablespoon sugar
1 teaspoon finely minced gingerroot
1 teaspoon salt, or to taste
Dash of ground white pepper

Prepare Ginger Dressing. In a large bowl, combine cabbage, carrot, sesame seeds, green onions and cilantro. Holding noodles over the salad bowl, break apart into small chunks and add to bowl. Mix in the dressing. With a spoon, cover noodle chunks with coleslaw mixture; refrigerate 8 hours to soften noodles and wilt cabbage. After 8 hours, press noodle chunks to separate. Stir in almonds. Serve at once or refrigerate until needed. Makes about 5 cups or 6 servings.

Ginger Dressing

In a small bowl, whisk together all ingredients. Makes about 3/4 cup.

Ripe Tomatoes Stuffed with Fresh Herb Vermicelli & Pine Nuts

Ripe garden tomatoes make this salad a special treat. The pasta is a showcase for the delicate flavor of the fresh herbs. A flavorful variation would be to toss the cooked, plain vermicelli with imported olive paste or fresh herb pesto.

4 medium to large tomatoes
2 tablespoons dairy sour cream
1 tablespoon rice vinegar
2 tablespoons extra-virgin olive oil
1 tablespoon marjoram leaves or minced fresh basil
1 tablespoon minced fresh parsley
2 teaspoons minced fresh chives
1/4 teaspoon salt
1 cup cooked vermicelli
2 tablespoons freshly grated pecorino Romano or Parmesan cheese
2 tablespoons toasted pine nuts
Fresh herb sprigs

In a large pot of boiling water, blanch tomatoes 10 seconds. Immediately transfer to a bowl of iced water. Peel tomatoes. With a small sharp knife, hollow out the centers of the tomatoes to form tomato cups. In a medium-size bowl, combine sour cream, rice vinegar, olive oil, herbs and salt. Toss vermicelli with dressing. Mix in cheese. Spoon mixture into tomato cups. Garnish with pine nuts and herbs. Makes 4 servings.

Garden Salad with Crispy Won-Ton Vermicelli & Olive Vinaigrette

Crisp threads of fried noodle wrappers dusted with Parmesan cheese enhance the flavor and texture of this refreshing salad. The distinctive-flavored dressing contains an imported Italian paste of olives, herbs, vinegar and other ingredients.

Crispy Won-Ton Vermicelli (page 12), using 4 ounces noodle wrappers
Olive Vinaigrette, see below
4 cups torn green leaf lettuce
4 cups torn romaine lettuce
1/2 cup slivered red onion
4 ounces crumbled mild goat cheese such as montrachet, or feta cheese

Olive Vinaigrette:

2 tablespoons red-wine vinegar
1 teaspoon Dijon-style mustard
1 garlic clove, finely minced
1/4 teaspoon salt
Pinch of freshly ground pepper
1 tablespoon Italian ripe or green olive paste
6 tablespoons extra-virgin olive oil or safflower oil

Prepare Crispy Won-Ton Vermicelli. Prepare Olive Vinaigrette. Combine lettuces and onion in a large salad bowl. Toss lightly with vinaigrette. Sprinkle each serving with goat cheese and a handful of fried vermicelli. Makes 4 servings.

Olive Vinaigrette

In a small bowl, mix vinegar, mustard, garlic, salt, pepper and olive paste. Whisk in oil until ingredients are well blended. Makes about 1/2 cup.

Smoked Chicken, Broccoli & Pine Nuts with Fried Rice Noodles

Deep-fried rice noodles are a crunchy, delicious addition to this colorful salad. Their texture and flavor add a touch of drama, especially if you fry them in front of your guests. Roasted chicken breasts from the deli will give you a head start in preparing this salad. Cooked shrimp or shredded Chinese roast duck can be substituted for the chicken.

Jade Cilantro Dressing (page 51)
2 ounces rice vermicelli or bean threads
1 cup vegetable oil for deep-frying
2 cups broccoli flowerets, blanched 1 minute, chilled in iced water and drained
1 medium-size red or yellow bell pepper, cut into 1/2-inch pieces
1/2 cup sliced water chestnuts
2 smoked or plain roasted chicken breast halves, boned, sliced
3 tablespoons toasted pine nuts

Prepare Jade Cilantro Dressing; set aside. Place noodles in a large grocery bag. Tear noodles apart into small bunches. In a wok or heavy, medium-size skillet, heat oil to 375°F (190°C). Test oil; if hot enough, a rice noodle will puff up and turn white within seconds. Fry noodles in small portions. Turn and fry second sides. Drain on a paper towel-lined baking sheet. In a large bowl, combine broccoli, bell pepper and water chestnuts. Measure 3 cups fried noodles. Gently combine with vegetable mixture. Spoon salad onto serving plates. Arrange slices of chicken on salads. Sprinkle dressing on top; garnish with pine nuts. Makes 2 main-dish salads or 4 first-course servings.

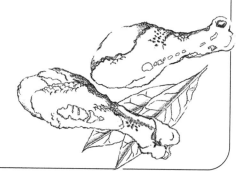

Crispy Chicken Salad with Smoky Hoisin Dressing

Crispy rice noodles, fried noodle strips and cashews create a triple explosion of flavor with every bite! The lightly-smoked Hoisin Dressing adds an intriguing flavor to this delicious main-dish salad. Roast duck or Cornish hens would be an excellent alternative to chicken.

Smoky Hoisin Dressing, see below
1 recipe Crispy Won-Ton Vermicelli (page 12), using 4 ounces noodle wrappers
1 ounce rice vermicelli or bean threads
Vegetable oil for deep-frying
1 (2- to 2-1/2-lb.) smoked chicken or barbecued chicken, shredded
5 cups shredded leaf lettuce
3 green onions, shredded diagonally
1 small red bell pepper, cut into julienne strips
1 small cucumber, seeded, cut into julienne strips
1/3 cup roasted cashew nuts, coarsely chopped

Smoky Hoisin Dressing:

2 tablespoons hoisin sauce
1/3 cup rice vinegar
6 tablespoons safflower oil
1 teaspoon chile-garlic sauce
1/4 cup sugar
1/2 teaspoon salt
2 teaspoons soy sauce
1/4 teaspoon liquid smoke

Prepare Smoky Hoisin Dressing. Prepare Crispy Won-Ton Vermicelli; omit Parmesan cheese. Put rice noodles in a paper bag; break apart. In a wok or deep skillet, heat oil to 375°F (190°C). Test oil; if hot enough, a rice noodle will puff up and turn white within seconds. Fry rice noodles in small portions. Turn and fry a few seconds on the other sides. Drain on a paper towel-lined baking sheet. In a large bowl, combine chicken, lettuce, green onions, bell pepper and cucumber. Toss in noodle vermicelli and rice noodles. Divide mixture among serving plates; garnish with cashew nuts. Spoon on dressing. Makes 4 or 5 main-dish servings.

Smoky Hoisin Dressing

Put all ingredients in a food processor with the metal blade. Process 15 seconds or until well blended. Makes about 1 cup.

Sesame-Almond Noodles

This pretty, crunchy noodle salad features Chinese-style instant ramen noodles which were popularized in Japan. The ingredients are versatile; omit shrimp and substitute strips of cooked chicken, beef or Chinese Roast Pork (page 42). The noodles can be cooked several hours ahead. Add remaining ingredients and dressing up to 30 minutes before serving.

Sesame Dressing, see below
1-1/2 cups finely shredded purple cabbage
Salt
2 (3-1/2-oz.) packages chicken-flavored instant ramen (plus 1 enclosed seasoning packet)
12 ounces medium-size shrimp, cooked, peeled, deveined and diced
2 or 3 thin green onions, smashed flat, then shredded
1/3 cup slivered toasted almonds
2 tablespoons cilantro, shredded

Sesame Dressing:

1/3 cup rice vinegar
1/4 cup vegetable oil
2 tablespoons sugar
1 garlic clove, finely minced
2 teaspoons soy sauce
1 teaspoon sesame oil
2 teaspoons hot chile paste
1 tablespoon toasted sesame seeds

Prepare Sesame Dressing; set aside. Place shredded cabbage in a large bowl; salt lightly. Set aside to wilt slightly. In a large pot, bring 1 quart water to a boil; add soup seasoning packet and ramen. Cook 2 minutes or just until noodles separate yet are firm to the bite. Do not overcook. Drain noodles in a colander; rinse under cool water. Drain well. In a large bowl, toss noodles with remaining ingredients. Add enough dressing to coat noodles. Serve at once. Makes 6 servings.

Sesame Dressing

In a medium-size bowl, whisk together all ingredients. Makes about 3/4 cup.

Chilled Buckwheat Noodles with Roasted Tomatoes & Fresh Herbs

The noodles are Japanese; the flavor is Italian. Hearty soba is so nutritious that certain Buddhist sects live on little besides soba and fresh fruit. In Japan, during the quiet hours of the night, the noodle vendor travels about pulling a little noodle kitchen on wheels. He blows a special horn to announce his arrival.

3 large ripe tomatoes
2 large garlic cloves, minced
1/4 cup minced fresh basil or oregano
2 tablespoons minced fresh parsley
1/4 cup extra-virgin olive oil
2 tablespoons balsamic vinegar
1/4 cup ripe Greek olives, chopped
1/2 teaspoon salt
Freshly ground pepper to taste
8 ounces dried Japanese soba or thin dried whole-wheat noodles
1/3 cup toasted chopped walnuts

Preheat broiler. On a broiler pan, roast tomatoes until skins are blistered and slightly charred. Turn often with tongs. Cool; remove skins. Cut tomatoes in half; gently squeeze out seeds. Chop pulp coarsely; place into a large bowl with remaining ingredients except soba and walnuts. Set aside at room temperature 2 to 3 hours. In a large pot, bring 3 quarts water to a boil; add noodles. Cook 4 to 5 minutes or until tender yet slightly firm to the bite. Drain well; rinse under cool water. Drain again. Place in a large bowl. Mix tomato sauce with noodles. Sprinkle each serving with walnuts. Makes 2 main-dish servings or 4 first-course servings.

Rice Noodle Salad with Fried Tofu, Fresh Mint & Peanuts

Rice noodles have a bland taste and act as the perfect foil for the exciting medley of flavors and textures in this Southeast Asian salad. You can add other interesting Oriental herbs and vegetables such as bean sprouts, enoki mushrooms, kaiwari daikon sprouts or shiso (perilla) leaves.

Vietnamese Chile-Lime Dressing (page 16)
6 ounces rice vermicelli, soaked in warm water 5 minutes, drained
1/2 carrot, cut into shreds
1 small cucumber, seeded and cut into shreds
1 large egg, cooked into a flat pancake and cut into shreds
1/4 cup minced mint leaves
1 (16-oz.) package firm Chinese-style tofu, rinsed
1/4 cup vegetable oil
1/4 cup cornstarch, more if needed
1/4 cup cilantro leaves, torn
1/3 cup chopped roasted peanuts

Prepare Vietnamese Chile-Lime Dressing. In a medium-size pot, bring 2 quarts water to a boil; add vermicelli. Cook 2 minutes or until tender yet still firm to the bite. Drain and rinse with cool water. Drain again; press out excess water. Toss noodles in a large bowl with carrot, cucumber, egg shreds and mint. Cut tofu horizontally into thin slices. Lay slices between double layers of kitchen towels or several layers of paper towels. With your hands, press tofu to squeeze out excess liquid. Continue blotting until fairly dry. Cut tofu into small cubes. In a wok or large nonstick skillet, heat oil over medium-high heat. Sift cornstarch over tofu cubes, turning to coat evenly. Add to hot oil and sauté 3 to 4 minutes or until all sides are golden-brown. Drain on paper towels. Place rice noodle salad on a large platter. Top with fried tofu, cilantro and chopped peanuts. Serve with dressing. Makes 4 servings.

Ingredients & Equipment

Oriental Wheat-Flour Noodles

This is not a complete list of all the types of noodles and pasta; just those featured in this book.

Soba: Japan: *soba,* Korea: *Naeng myon.* Japanese soba is a brownish-grey, slightly coarse noodle made from buckwheat flour and wheat flour. It is popular in Tokyo and Northern Japan where buckwheat is a cold-weather crop. Korean soba is made from buckwheat and potato starch or cornstarch. Naeng myon is lighter-colored and has a chewier consistency than Japanese soba. Soba is eaten with dipping sauce in the summertime. In Japan, it is used in rolled vegetarian sushi. In the winter, it is served in bowls of hot broth, often with toppings of tempura, fried tofu, sliced beef, pickles or vegetables. Japanese soba is also made in green tea, mushroom, egg and mountain yam flavors. Purchase soba in Asian markets and health food stores.

Udon: *Nama udon,* or fresh udon, are thick, chewy, white wheat noodles favored in Southern Japan and Kyoto. They can be made from whole wheat or a combination of whole wheat and bleached white flour. Udon resembles spaghetti but also comes in flat noodles. It is available pre-cooked in packages with sauce packets, frozen and dried. Udon is not traditionally served in cold dishes. It is a popular winter food served in rich stews and one-pot dishes. They can be stir-fried, and added to soup broth. Skilled noodle makers in Japan sometimes knead the dough by foot.

Kishimen: A Nagoya specialty, these wheat noodles are similar to udon but flatter and wider, like fettuccine. Purchase the noodles dried; prepare and serve like udon.

Hiyamugi: A vermicelli-type wheat noodle similar to somen but slightly larger. It is eaten in cold dishes in the summertime. You will recognize them if you look for a few pink and green noodles tucked into each package.

Somen: A fine, delicate vermicelli-like wheat noodle made from a dough made with sesame oil. The cooked noodles are mainly served in water with ice cubes during the summer. In Southern Japan and Chinese-influenced Okinawa, somen is stir-fried with meat and vegetables. Pretty pink, plum-flavored somen is available as well as sunny yellow somen with egg and green tea somen. Sometimes somen is tied at one end before cooking to keep all the noodles flowing one way in the finished dish.

Egg Noodles

Chinese Egg Noodles: Chinese: *dan mein,* Thai: *ba-mee,* Vietnamese: *mee,* Indonesian: *mie,* Korean: *son-myon.* Egg noodles are made from wheat flour and egg. In large Chinese markets, special noodles are flavored with spinach, shrimp roe or chicken stock. Egg noodles are available fresh, frozen and dried in Asian markets. Use for stir-fried mixtures, soups or fried noodle cakes topped with saucy meat, seafood and vegetable toppings. The Chinese generally use two sizes of noodles: ribbon-shaped noodles which range from 1/8 to 1/4 inch wide and shoelace-thin noodles, about 1/16 inch wide. Substitute Italian dried fettuccine or linguini for the wide noodles and dried spaghettini for the thin noodles.

Pale-colored Chinese water noodles, or chow-mein noodles, are made without egg. Water-noodle dough is used for making hand-pulled noodles. Use water-noodles in stir-fry dishes, soups or mix with sauce. Purchase in markets or make your own with the recipe on page 8. You can substitute egg noodles or dried spaghettini. Korean son myon are thin wheat noodles. You can substitute Japanese kishimen, hiyamugi or somen.

Ramen: This Chinese-style noodle from Japan is made from a special wheat flour and an alkali water that creates its characteristic texture. Tinted yellow and eggless, ramen sometimes contains lard, resulting in a richer flavor than traditional Japanese soba or udon. Ramen is mainly used in a variety of soups and soup-stews. Purchase fresh or fresh-frozen in Asian markets. Fresh commercial ramen needs little cooking. Drop into a large pot of boiling water 30 seconds to refresh the taste. Rinse in cold water; drain well. Add to hot soups or toss with a flavorful sauce to make a tasty snack or salad.

Instant Ramen: Japanese instant ramen is extruded rather than machine cut. It is deep-fried or steamed and dry-packaged for quick rehydration and consumption. Look for cup-style noodles or small square paper-wrapped packets of the dried noodles. Each serving comes with a foil packet of soup mix in chicken, pork, miso, seafood or Oriental flavors. Health food stores carry high-quality, steamed, instant ramen packets.

Yaki Soba: A type of ramen used for stir-fried Japanese noodle dishes. Available fresh or fresh-frozen in Asian markets. Good for soups and cold dishes too.

Chuka Soba: A type of ramen which is precooked, then dried into bundles of tight curly noodles. Cook 2 to 3 minutes before use. Good for stir-fry dishes, soups and cold dishes. When stir-fried, the noodles are called chuka-mein.

Rice Noodles

Dried Rice Vermicelli: China: *mai fun,* Thailand: *sen mee,* Malaysia: *mee hoon,* Vietnamese: *bun,* Indonesian: *be-hun.* Rice vermicelli or rice sticks are thin wirelike noodles about 1/32 inch wide. Soak in warm water 5 minutes; simmer 1 minute in a pan of boiling water. Simmer less time if they are to be stir-fried. After rinsing noodles, gently press out excess water. Discard clumps which won't separate. Rice vermicelli breaks up naturally after soaking. Good in soups, cold dishes and with grilled meats. Dried rice noodles also come in larger round or flat sizes. They must be cooked 3 to 4 minutes after soaking. Add to soups, stir-fries and cold noodle dishes. Presoaking improves flavor and texture and removes excess starch. Unsoaked rice noodles can be deep-fried. They puff up dramatically, increasing in size. Use one ounce per person for a salad serving or 2 ounces per person for a main serving.

Fresh Rice Noodles: Thai: *kway-tio,* Chinese: *sha-he-fen.* These soft, chewy noodles are made from glutinous rice flour. They are steamed, coated with oil, then folded into square sheets. When added to dishes, they soak up seasonings and sauces as they are cooked. Cut the sheets into strips before use.

Before using packaged rice noodles in recipes, cover briefly with boiling water to freshen them and remove excess oil. Cook briefly; noodles overcook easily. Refrigerate fresh noodles 2 or 3 days. If the edges become too firm to use; steam briefly to soften. Fresh rice noodles are often used as wrappers. In Chinatown, fresh rice noodles are steamed with seasonings such as green onion, Chinese sausage, dried shrimp or sesame seeds. Look for rice noodles in markets near large Asian communities. If you can't find them, try the recipe on page 3 for a good substitute.

Rice-Paper Wrappers: Translucent rice papers, or *bánh tráng,* are made from cooked rice dough and shaped into thin circular or triangular pieces. The sheets become imprinted with a basketweave design when dried on bamboo mats. To soften before use, dip wrappers into water or brush with beaten egg. Shake off all excess water; use immediately when softened. Softened wrappers can be filled and deep-fried. For fresh spring rolls, layer with lettuce and stir-fried filling, roll up and eat. Store dry wrappers in an airtight container.

Vegetable Noodles

Mung Bean Noodles: Chinese: *fun-si* (powdered silk), Japanese: *harusame* (spring rain), Thai: *woon sen, Vietnamese: bun,* Philippines: *sotanghon,* Korean: *tang-myon* or *dang-myon.* These wiry strands are a vegetable product made generally from mung beans, potato starch or sweet-potato starch. They are known by several names: bean threads, pea-starch noodles, glass noodles, silver noodles, cellophane noodles or long rice *(sai-fun).* The noodles are tough and must be cut with scissors. Soften in warm water 20 minutes. Simmer 10 minutes; simmer 5 minutes if noodles are to be cooked again. Soaked noodles resemble translucent gelatin strings. The chewy noodles absorb other food flavors. Unsoaked noodles can be deep-

fried. They become white and crunchy, expanding in size dramatically. Purchase bean threads in a pink-net wrapped bundle of individual 2-ounce packages. Koreans add snipped soaked noodles to dumpling fillings. Add to won-ton or spring-roll fillings to absorb excess moisture. A fried bean thread nest is a stunning bed for any stir-fried dish. A 2-ounce bundle of bean threads yields about 2 cups soaked noodles. Use about 1-1/2 ounces for each salad portion; use 3 ounces for each main serving.

Noodle Wrappers

Spring Roll Wrappers: Shanghai spring roll wrappers are paper-thin round or square skins about 7 inches in diameter. They are made from flour and water dough that is cooked on a griddle. They are very delicate and crispy when deep-fried. Shanghai wrappers can be steamed and rolled with savory fillings. **Filipino lumpia wrappers** are similar to Shanghai wrappers. If Shanghai wrappers or lumpia wrappers seem too dry, steam briefly to make them more pliable. These wrappers are available, usually frozen, in Oriental markets. **Cantonese spring roll wrappers** (egg roll wrappers) are made from noodle dough with egg. They are thicker, and more dense than the fried Shanghai wrappers. If they seem too thick for your taste, make them thinner by running them through the roller of a pasta machine with the notch turned to the last setting (7). Dust with cornstarch to facilitate rolling. Trim into 6-inch or 7-inch squares.

Won-Ton Wrappers: Won-ton wrappers are made from the same noodle dough used for Cantonese spring roll wrappers. They are cut into 3-inch squares. The thinnest won-ton wrappers are available in Asian markets. Thicker wrappers sold in American markets are fine, but they can be rolled thinner in a pasta machine. Trim to 3-inch squares. Exciting new colorful won-ton wrappers made from carrot, beet and spinach are now available in certain areas of the country. Store up to 10 days in the refrigerator or freeze for longer storage.

Italian Pasta

This is not a complete list of pasta, only those mentioned in this book.

STRINGS

Bucatini: Thicker than spaghetti, this pasta has a hollow center.

Spaghetti: Round, thin pasta. One of the most common pastas served in Italy, but rarely with meat sauce or meatballs. Most popular are quick sauces based on tomatoes, white sauces or olive oil and garlic.

Spaghettini: Thin spaghetti

Vermicelli: Spaghetti thinner than spaghettini.

Cappellini: Very fine spaghetti; similar to angel hair pasta.

Cappelli d'Angelo: angel hair; the finest spaghetti.

RIBBONS

Tagliatelle: The Bolognese term for the ribbon-shaped egg noodles similar to fettuccine, but slightly thinner and slightly wider. The two are interchangeable. In Bologna, tagliatelle is favored with meat sauce.

Fettuccine: This is the Roman name for long, narrow egg noodles which range from 1/8 inch wide to 1/4 inch wide. Similar to tagliatelle, though slightly thicker and more narrow. Popular in Italy with creamy sauces.

Pappardelle: Wide noodles cut slightly more than 1/2 inch wide. They have a fluted edge. Cut strips of pappardelle from noodle dough rolled by hand.

Linguini: Flat spaghetti about 1/8 inch wide.

Tagliarini: Egg noodles cut thinner than linguini, about 1/16 inch wide. For homemade tagliarini, roll the dough as thin as possible; cut with the narrow blade of a pasta machine. These won't be quite as flat as some commercially made kinds.

Fusilli: Short, thin corkscrew shapes or fatter spiral shapes. Long fusilli looks like spaghetti with a corkscrew shape.

Gemelli: This pasta looks like two short pieces of spaghetti twisted together.

Other Ingredients

All-Purpose Flour: Bleached all-purpose and unbleached all-purpose flour are excellent for making tender egg noodles. They contain just enough gluten to create an elastic dough that is easy to roll out by hand. Use dough for Chinese and Italian egg noodles, Chinese egg-roll wrappers and won-ton wrappers. Swansdown® cake flour is the preferred brand of soft wheat flour among Chinese home cooks for making "rice noodles."

Brown Bean Sauce: This thick flavorful Chinese sauce is sometimes called yellow bean sauce. It is made from salted fermented whole or ground soybeans. **Hot Bean Sauce** is a similar chunky-textured dark brown sauce made of soybeans, garlic and hot chiles. These sauces can add flavor, body and heat to sauces and marinades. Store in airtight containers in the refrigerator almost indefinitely.

Buckwheat Flour: Buckwheat flour has a hearty robust flavor. It is especially nutritious, rich in calcium, vitamin E and the vitamin B-complex. Buckwheat is ground from seeds and contains no gluten. Soft buckwheat flour needs to be combined with gluten flour to create a dough with suitable elasticity. Japanese *soba* is the most well known buckwheat flour noodle. China, Korea and Italy also eat buckwheat noodles.

Cheeses: Parmesan cheese, made from cow's milk, is a delicious hard grating cheese. Parmigiano-Reggiano, a Northern Italian favorite, is the true Italian Parmesan. Its extraordinary flavor is slightly sweet, almost nutty. Other similar less-expensive, Italian grating cheeses (collectively known as *grana*) are available in American markets. Southern Italians enjoy **pecorino**, a slightly salty, distinctive-flavored cheese made from sheep's milk. It can be found under the names, Grating Pecorino and Pecorino Romano. Another choice is **Dry Monterey Jack** (Dry Jack), a fine aged cheese with a sweet nutty taste, much like Parmesan. Grate cheeses as needed to protect their distinctive flavors and aromas. Avoid domestic Parmesan and Romano sold in jars and cardboard containers. **Mozzarella** is highly valued in the Naples region of Campania. Once made from water buffalo milk, it is now made primarily from cow's milk. Purchase in soft, moist, creamy, 1-pound ovals.

Chile Peppers: Chiles are high in vitamins A and C. To add raw heat to foods, use jalapeño peppers, smaller Serrano chiles or the tiny, fiery-hot "bird" chiles favored in Thai cuisine. Do not peel these chiles. Remove seeds to tame the heat. Ground chiles come in several forms including fiery-hot cayenne pepper, Korean coarsely ground chile powder (kochu) and pure New Mexican ground chile powder, which can vary in heat.

Chile Sauce: Hot chile sauce adds flavor as well as heat to foods. Use with discretion; one teaspoon will add heavy fire-power. My favorites are Thai **Sriracha Hot Chile Sauce®**, made from sun-ripened red serrano chiles, garlic and vinegar and

Vietnamese Chili-Garlic Sauce® made by Huy Fong Foods, Inc., Los Angeles. To recognize the latter, look for the plastic container with a green lid and a rooster on the front. Indonesian **sambal ulek** is another favorite hot sauce. A favorite Chinese blend is **Chili (Chilli) Paste with Garlic®** by Lan Chi. These are available in Asian markets. Store almost indefinitely in the refrigerator.

Cilantro: Fresh coriander. Also known as Chinese parsley. One of the oldest known herbs. The leaves resemble flat-leaf parsley. There is no substitute for cilantro's distinctive flavor. It is increasingly available in supermarkets and readily available in Asian and Latin markets. Refrigerate in an airtight plastic bag. Do not use dried cilantro; the flavor is lost.

Chinese Sausage: These rich-tasting, slightly sweet dried sausages come in links. Steam to soften before slicing, if desired. Add to your favorite noodle dishes. Sausages can be frozen.

Chikuwa: These hollow, cooked fish rolls are part of a group of surimi-based foods in Japan known as *neri-seihin*. Chikuwa, or "bamboo wheel," was the original form made from fish paste shaped around bamboo stalks, then grilled. Purchase in refrigerator or freezer sections of Oriental markets. Chikuwa has an elastic, chewy texture and a mild fish taste. Delicious added to noodle stir-fries, noodle soups, and one-pot dishes such as nabeyaki udon (page 52).

Cumin: Cumin seeds are believed to have originated in the Middle East and are also used in Mediterranean, Indian, Spanish, Latin American and Southeast Asian cuisines. The seeds have an earthy, wonderful flavor. When grinding the seeds, toast first to enhance their flavor.

Cornstarch: Cornstarch produces satiny smooth, translucent sauces, velvetizes meat textures through marination and seals in food's natural juices in deep-frying. Cornstarch has twice the thickening power of flour. Dissolve in cool liquids; stir and boil 1 full minute. This helps prevent weeping, removes the starchy taste and expands starch molecules for maximum thickening power. Always reblend uncooked cornstarch mixtures just before stirring them into your foods.

Curry Paste: Curry paste is a heady blend of herbs and spices. Use to flavor stir-fry dishes, noodle dishes, soups and curries. Red, green and yellow Thai curry pastes are available in Asian markets. Good-quality Indian curry paste is available in Asian and Indian markets. The pastes offer a more complex range of dynamic flavors than dried powder.

Fish Sauce: Thin, light-brown, salty fermented fish sauce is used extensively as a seasoning in Vietnam (*nuoc-mam*), Thailand (*nam pla*), the Philippines (patis) and other Southeast Asian countries. It is used much the same way soy sauce is used. It adds flavor depth and enhances natural flavor of foods without leaving a fishy taste.

Five-Spice Power: Ground spice mixture which usually includes star anise, cinnamon, Szechwan peppercorns, cloves and fennel among other spices. Use in sauces and marinades.

Garlic: Select firm, heavy large heads of garlic, preferably like those found at farmers' markets or in Asian markets. Smash garlic cloves with the flat side of a cleaver or large chef's knife to loosen the skins for easy removal and to flatten for mincing. Garlic mellows as it cooks, adding a wonderful flavor. Store in a cool dry place. Do not substitute garlic powder or garlic salt.

Gingerroot: A gnarled, spicy-tasting root indispensable to Asian cuisine. Peel or scrape off outer brown skin with a vegetable peeler or small paring knife. Young spring ginger doesn't need peeling. Ground ginger is not an acceptable substitute. Buy small amounts of fresh firm gingerroot; store in a cool place. I like to buy extra pieces to plant in pots of sandy soil. The ginger will push forth attractive, tall green shoots which resemble bamboo shoots.

Hoisin Sauce: Thick, sweet, dark commercial Chinese sauce made from fermented soybeans, sugar, garlic, vinegar, chiles and spices. Used in Chinese barbecue sauce, stir-fries, marinades and sauces. Refrigerate after opening.

Kamaboko: Fish cake loaves are part of a group of surimi-based foods in Japan. Surimi is mixed with starch, mirin and other ingredients, then shaped and steamed. The loaves are formed on rectangular wooden boards. Some are coated with pink color. The chewy texture is an especially desirable quality. Purchase in the refrigerator or freezer section of Oriental markets. Slices of kamaboko can be added to noodle soups and stews. Strips can be added to noodle stir-fries, fritter batters and noodle dishes of soba and udon.

Korean Bean Paste: *Kochu jang,* a brick-colored bean paste, is made from ground red chiles, glutinous rice flour and soybean paste. The slightly sweet, spicy condiment is an essential ingredient in the Korean kitchen. Stir it into soups, dips, marinades and salad dressings. **Roasted hot bean paste** is a similar hot-sweet condiment with small bits of fermented soybeans.

Lemon Grass: Tall green stalks of grass with an aromatic citrus-lemon flavor. Peel away dry outer leaves of each stalk to reach the tender, inner portion inside. Smash and slice the inner stalk, then mince finely. Add to Southeast Asian marinades, soups, braised dishes, spice pastes and stir-fried dishes. Lemon grass has a special flavor, but grated fresh lemon peel or minced fresh lemon balm are good substitutes.

Miso: Japanese fermented soybean paste. Resembles peanut butter in consistency but is available in a variety of colors, textures, flavors and aromas. Three basic types are rice miso, soybean miso and barley miso.

Oyster Sauce: A mild, rich-tasting thick brown sauce made from oyster extracts. Lee Kum Kee is an excellent Hong Kong brand. Adds flavor depth to sauces, soups and stir-fry dishes.

Pancetta: This unsmoked, flavorful Italian bacon can be purchased in Italian markets or upscale food shops. It comes in round or oval shapes. Slice, chop or dice and sauté like bacon. You can substitute bacon; blanch first in boiling water to remove smoky taste.

Rice Flour: This starchy Asian flour is ground from sweet glutinous rice and is used to make dried rice noodles, dumpling wrappers and fresh rice noodles. Look for boxes of Japanese rice flour labeled *mochiko*.

Rice Vinegar: Naturally fermented clear rice vinegar is made from white rice. It has a mild flavor and natural sweetness. Excellent for preparing dishes from all cuisines.

Semolina Flour: Ground from durum wheat, this golden flour produces a strong, resilient dough that is difficult for the home cook to roll to the proper thinness by hand. Semolina is always used in commercial noodles and pasta.

Sesame Oil: Aromatic, amber-colored oil pressed from toasted sesame seeds. High amounts of vitamin E helps stabilize the oil. It is rarely used as a cooking oil because it burns at high temperatures, destroying its special flavor. Add sparingly to marinades and sauces. Sprinkle a small amount into noodle dishes in the final seconds of cooking.

Sesame Seeds: Sesame seeds are abundant in protein, vitamins, calcium and phosphorous. White-hulled sesame seeds or black sesame seeds are good for garnishing. Less expensive unhulled, mottled seeds can be used for grinding into pastes. Toast sesame seeds in a small pan over medium heat until lightly browned and aromatic. Shake pan often to prevent burning.

Shiitake Mushrooms: Flavorful, earthy-tasting mushrooms. Available fresh or dried. Soak dried mushrooms in hot water 20 minutes or longer to soften. Trim and discard tough stems. The flavorful water can be added to soups and sauces.

Shiso Leaves: Or *perilla*, the bright-green leaf of the beefsteak plant. It has a distinctive, slightly minty flavor. Popular in Japanese cuisine, shiso is delicious added to chilled noodle dishes. It is worth cultivating in your garden.

Soy Sauce: A naturally fermented, dark, salty liquid made from soybeans, *koji* (a mold) and water. Light-colored, thin soy sauce is very salty. Japanese soy sauce (thin or medium) works best for Japanese cuisine but can be used successfully in either Korean, Chinese or Western dishes. Japanese *tamari* is brewed strictly from soybeans with no wheat added. It is available in health food stores. Chinese soy sauce is excellent; in Asian markets look for light soy sauce or dark mushroom soy sauce.

Star Anise: Star-shaped fruit of a small evergreen tree. The spice has eight-points; each contain a seed. Adds a delicious licorice-flavor to broths, sauces, meats, poultry, pork and fish. The seasoned meats add an elusive flavor to noodle dishes. The ground spice is a main ingredient in five-spice powder.

Sun-dried Tomato: Sun-dried tomatoes have a concentrated tangy-sweet flavor. Rehydrate three ounces by simmering in 1-1/2 cups water over low heat two minutes. Remove from heat; tomatoes will plump up within 30 minutes. Press out excess liquid. Use in recipes or store in olive oil with herbs in the refrigerator. Three ounces of sun-dried tomatoes equal about 1-1/4 cups rehydrated tomatoes.

Surimi: Surimi, or "minced meat," is a homogeneous protein gel or fish paste developed by an ancient Japanese process. In American markets, the most common form is surimi seafood analog or "imitation seafood." Faux crab, scallops, shrimp and lobster all look and taste similar to the real thing. Surimi is low in cholesterol and fat and high in essential amino acids. A 100-gram serving averages less than 100 calories and as many as 13 grams of protein. See *chikuwa* and *kamaboko*.

Szechuan Peppercorns: Spicy berries from the prickly ash tree. Also known in China as *fagara pepper,* or flower pepper. Dried, the berries are ground into a pepperlike seasoning that gives a flavor boost to most noodle dishes.

Tree Ears: Also known as cloud ears, this small tree fungus is valued for its texture. The flavor is very mild. Soak the dried chips in hot water until rehydrated. Trim off hard spots. Rinse several times to remove grit.

Tofu: Blocks of solid custardlike food made from coagulated soybean milk. Extra-firm Chinese tofu is excellent for stir-frying. Slightly less-firm Japanese tofu can be fried; press between paper towels to remove excess moisture first. Japanese *kinogoshi*, or custard tofu, is best cut into cubes and eaten with dipping sauce or added to soups. It can be pureed for salad dressings, sauces and other soft-textured dishes. Refrigerate in water; change daily. Best used within one or two days.

Vegetable Oils: Peanut oil is good for deep-frying because it can be heated to higher temperatures without breaking down chemically. Freshen cooking oil by deep-frying three or four slices of fresh gingerroot until they turn light brown. **Corn oil** is excellent for Oriental stir-frying or deep-frying. **Safflower oil** is highly unsaturated and is excel-lent for stir-frying and for salad dressings. **Olive oil** comes in a range of aromas, colors and tastes. Top-quality extra-virgin oil is from the first cold pressing. Quality varies depending on the quality of the olives. Reserve the finest oils for simple dishes requiring little or no cooking. These are suitable for use as a condiment or sauce. Full-bodied virgin oils are from subsequent pressings; use for hearty salads, meat and pasta dishes and for sautéing. **Hot chile oil** is made by frying chile pepper flakes in vegetable oil. Add paprika for color. Strain out the pepper flakes. Bottle and store in a cool place.

Wines: Vermouth is an excellent dry white wine for many kitchen uses including marinades, poaching and sauces. **Mirin** is a slightly syrupy Japanese rice wine made from sweet glutinous rice, a starter mold and distilled 90 proof liquor, or *shochu*. It is indispensable to Japanese cuisine, adding sweetness and an attractive glaze to foods. Top-quality **dry sherry** is a good substitute for Chinese rice wine. Dry vermouth will sometimes work. Never use cooking wines from the grocery store. If wines are unsuitable for drinking, do not use in cooking.

Recommended Cooking Equipment

Cheese Grater: A necessary piece of equipment for grating chunks of hard cheese such as Parmesan or pecorino Romano.

Chinese Spatula: An excellent aid for stir-frying. The wide sturdy spatula stirs food, turns it and can be used to press and flatten it in the pan.

Chinese Wire Strainer: This is one of the handiest tools in my kitchen. The large strainer looks like a round piece of concave chicken wire on a handle. It is a handy tool to use for any cuisine. I use it to lower foods into hot oil for cooking, then to remove them from the oil. It is useful for scooping noodles and dumplings from boiling water.

Colander: A large metal colander is useful and convenient for draining cooked noodles.

Donburi: These large, deep Japanese pottery and porcelain bowls with matching lids are intended for one-bowl rice meals. They are also perfect for individual portions of Japanese noodles. Larger Japanese lacquer noodle bowls are available in Asian markets and gift stores.

Dough Scraper: This is a wonderful tool for scraping flour and dough from the work surface. Great for quick clean-up.

Noodle Duster: To create an instant starch-filled duster for dough and noodles, place cornstarch or flour inside a homemade cheesecloth bag and tie off the top. Or, place the starch in the middle of a clean handkerchief. Pull up the corners and tie in a knot. You could also use a large soft brush for dusting noodles.

Pasta Machine: Both manual and electric pasta machines are available for rolling and cutting pasta dough. The manual machine does an excellent job and saves much effort and time rolling noodle doughs.

Rolling Pin: A long thin wooden rolling pin, about three feet long and two inches in diameter, works best for rolling out noodle dough. Thin rolling pins are favored in Europe and in Asia. The American rolling pin with two handles is not the best choice. They are too thick and not long enough.

Wok: The concave shape of a wok allows the bottom to have direct contact with the heat source. This is ideal for stir-frying. Heat is evenly dispersed; foods will cook more efficiently as they are stirred. The wok is also good for pan-frying, deep-frying and steaming. Select a carbon steel wok which heats up fast and cools off quickly. A well-seasoned wok is crucial. Less oil will be required for stir-frying; foods such as meats or noodles will not stick. When stir-frying, heat the wok before the oil is added. Pour in the oil; roll pan around to coat the bottom. This will help prevent sticking. Before stir-frying, arrange all the measured ingredients on a tray. Once stir-frying begins, there is no time for additional preparation.

Index

Comparison to Metric Measure

When You Symbol Know	Symbol	Multiply By	To Find	
teaspoons	tsp	5.0	milliliters	ml
tablespoons	tbsp	15.0	milliliters	ml
fluid ounces	fl. oz.	30.0	milliliters	ml
cups	c	0.24	liters	l
pints	pt.	0.47	liters	l
quarts	qt.	0.95	liters	l
ounces	oz.	28.0	grams	g
pounds	lb.	0.45	kilograms	kg
Fahrenheit	F	5/9 (after	Celsius	C

Fahrenheit to Celsius

F	C
200—205	95
220—225	105
245—250	120
275	135
300—305	150
325—330	165
345—350	175
370—375	190
400—405	205
425—430	220
445—450	230
470—475	245
500	260

Liquid Measure to Milliliters

1/4 teaspoon	=	1.25 milliliters
1/2 teaspoon	=	2.5 milliliters
3/4 teaspoon	=	3.75 milliliters
1 teaspoon	=	5.0 milliliters
1-1/4 teaspoons	=	6.25 milliliters
1-1/2 teaspoons	=	7.5 milliliters
1-3/4 teaspoons	=	8.75 milliliters
2 teaspoons	=	10.0 milliliters
1 tablespoon	=	15.0 milliliters
2 tablespoons	=	30.0 milliliters

Liquid Measure to Liters

1/4 cup	=	0.06 liters
1/2 cup	=	0.12 liters
3/4 cup	=	0.18 liters
1 cup	=	0.24 liters
1-1/4 cups	=	0.3 liters
1-1/2 cups	=	0.36 liters
2 cups	=	0.48 liters
2-1/2 cups	=	0.6 liters
3 cups	=	0.72 liters
3-1/2 cups	=	0.84 liters
4 cups	=	0.96 liters
4-1/2 cups	=	1.08 liters
5 cups	=	1.2 liters
5-1/2 cups	=	1.32 liters